R.E.I. Editions

All of our ebooks can be read on the following devices:
- Computers
- eReaders
- iOS
- Android
- Blackberries
- Windows
- Tablet
- Cellular

Christian Valnet

Chromotherapy

The Power of Colors

ISBN: 978-2-37297-1645

Published: January 2015
New updated edition: January 2023
Copyright © 2015 - 2023 R.E.I. Editions
www.rei-editions.com

Christian Valnet

Chromotherapy

The Power of Colors

R.E.I. Editions

Indice

Chromotherapy

Able to act on all levels of our being (body, mind and spirit), color is endowed with energy which, if used correctly, has powerful calming, regenerative and harmonizing effects. Chromotherapy is an alternative medicine that uses colors as a therapy for the treatment of diseases. Chromotherapy is now counted among the so-called "alternative medicines". ancient civilizations exploited the meaning of colors and their effect on man's physical and psychic processes, with excellent results. In fact, chromotherapy has very ancient origins, since traditional medicines have always attributed great importance to the influence of colors on man's health and state of mind. Chromotherapy practices were known since Ancient Egypt: Egyptian mythology assigns the discovery of chromotherapy to the god Thoth. according to the hermetic tradition, both the Egyptians and the Greeks made use of minerals, stones, crystals and colored ointments, as well as painting the walls of the places of treatment. In Ancient Egypt, each color had a name that identified its "potential", i.e. its functionality:

- Black (KeM) was a symbol of fertility.
- Yellow (KeNiT), which is synonymous with "gold" as in alchemy, was a symbol of solar divinity (with a continuous radiation function).
- Red (DeSHeR) was a symbol of blood and fire, it could be a positive or negative energy, but it is always synonymous with extremism, going from the extreme hostility of the "desert" and "crazy" behavior to the greatest kindness, because a strong heart and regenerated blood are synonymous with good health and for the ancients, diseases were a symptom of vicious and perverse behavior (that is, disharmonious with the laws of the spirit and nature); in fact, the medicine was called PeKheReT (in whose hieroglyph the fermentation of bread and the intestinal viscera were symbolized) and the cure was magically prepared, where, by magic (HeKA),

9

we meant the primordial (causal) energy transcending this world and preceding to the very creation of the Neter. The remedy therefore had to "circulate" and spread harmoniously throughout the body.

In 1878, the American Edwin Babitt published his book "The principle of Light and Color", which had worldwide circulation and laid the foundation stone for modern chromotherapy. The doctor declared the importance of white light (sunlight) to live well: human beings, like plants, need light to survive and testified the change in appearance that the skin has when exposed to the sun, without excesses, becoming healthier, reducing impurities and assuming a rosy and healthy complexion. Today it has been demonstrated that sunlight acts on the metabolism by accelerating the activities of cells and all the processes of elimination of waste, absorption of useful substances and blood circulation: for this reason it helps against fever, colds and pains by acting deeply in the body and reactivating all tissues. By increasing sweating, more toxic substances are eliminated and with shorter light waves the destruction of bacteria is more effective. In more recent years, in 1920, the Indian colonel Dinshah Pestanji Framji Ghadiali invented "spectrochromotherapy", a therapy which provided for the use of different colored lights for each pathology, combined with dietary prescriptions. Ghandiali, who worked in the United States for over thirty years (during which he was also involved in several trials on charges of fraud), built the "spectrochrome", a machine which consisted of a strong light source in front of which they could be added color filters. He also published a voluminous three-volume encyclopedia entitled "Spectro-Chrome Metry Encyclopedia" and the monthly periodical entitled Spectro-Chrome. He was the first, and other researchers later, demonstrated the influence of colors on the glands: the secretion of each gland is stimulated by a different colour, increasing the concentration of the colour, the activity increases and the endocrine product spreads throughout the body until to interested parties. In particular, these gland/color associations were demonstrated:
- Liver - red.

- Pituitary - green.
- Thyroid - orange.
- Prostate - magenta.
- Ovaries - scarlet.

When we are attracted to certain colors in particular moments, according to chromotherapy it is because we lack the energy produced by those colours. The use of color not only has a therapeutic purpose but is even more effective if used for preventive purposes: in addition to not having the sometimes very serious side effects of traditional medicine and being able to be used as an anesthetic since it acts directly on the cause of the pain and not on the centers of the brain, it prepares the body to deal with problems faster and more focused. The color acts only on the area on which it is applied without interfering with what is around it, it takes care of the organs and stimulates the glands and the lymphatic system, favoring the expulsion of toxins and bacteria: the body thus remains more "pure" and eliminating harmful substances that can slow down the normal functions of the body is more reactive when it has to deal with infections or threats by dealing more effectively with ailments. The physicist and doctor of Scandinavian origin Oscar Brunler, after the commitment and the prizes won for his activity during the Second World War, decided to abandon physics to study medicine and in particular the application of chromotherapy: thanks to his research he was able to document numerous cases in which chromotherapy had a positive outcome faster and more effectively than official medicine. Using yellow-orange radiation on the liver of diabetics it was possible to reduce the daily amounts of insulin; with the same method he managed to make a group of men intoxicated by alcohol stop drinking, which did not happen to those who were irradiated with red. With the red light, however, he managed to remove the inflammation of an appendix in a few minutes without surgical intervention. He also reported some observed cases where patients wrapped in red blankets recovered faster: this method was used effectively in the Balkans to recover from smallpox and in India for post-operative recovery. Brunler explained these phenomena with the fact that colour, being a wave, is a

11

form of energy. When a body is irradiated, this energy activates and draws blood to the skin decreasing the congestion of the liver, spleen, lungs, stomach, intestines and spine and aiding its clearing and elimination from the organ of harmful residues. Even if the application is done on time, the whole body benefits from it. Less discussed predecessors of the previous one were the Italian Antonino Sciascia and the Danish Niels Finsen, pioneers of research on light. Both doctors and scientists, in 1892 and 1893, informed the academic world of their discoveries on phototherapy. Based on the demonstration of the results obtained with a technique for treating smallpox scars by exposure to light, Finsen pioneered medical studies on the real effects of light on the human body, and received the Nobel Prize in 1903 for his discoveries on phototherapy in the treatment of tuberculosis. The effectiveness of chromotherapy is contested by the scientific community, as no chromotherapy practice has ever been able to pass a controlled clinical study, which allows to verify its actual effectiveness. In the absence of such studies, single healing episodes do not constitute proof, as the intervention of external factors or the placebo effect cannot be excluded. The absence of proven results leads us to consider the theories underlying chromotherapy as mere hypotheses, which however are not supported by experimental evidence; moreover, the theoretical basis of chromotherapy is considered rather fragile: even if colors can have effects on the psychological state of an individual, the extension of these effects to the treatment of the most varied diseases is not supported by any current knowledge on the nature of light or on human physiology.

Even the results obtained by Niels Finsen in the field of phototherapy are difficult to extend to chromotherapy practices, as they concern the entire electromagnetic spectrum, and not just visible light, and are mainly based on the bactericidal properties of light. Furthermore, phototherapy treatments are no longer used today because they have been surpassed in effectiveness by antibiotics, even if they have given impetus to radiotherapy and sterilization using ultraviolet light. For these reasons, chromotherapy is classified under pseudoscience. Raymond Twyeffort, an American, in 1930 managed to solve many of his problems related to phobias and gastric pains by realizing that by wearing a red jacket he perceived a new energy and new enthusiasm. He therefore began to experiment with brightly colored and always different fashion elements and each one helped him to overcome his psychophysical situation. He made this intuition his distinctive character by creating different elements of men's fashion. The stylist who understood colors. In recent years, chromotherapy has had a remarkable development thanks to the numerous scientific studies that highlight the influence of colors on the nervous, immune and metabolic systems. Chromotherapy is an integrative medicine (it easily integrates with other therapies or treatments to enhance the result) which uses colors to help the body and mind regain their natural balance. Assuming that our body is crossed by different energy points, it has been seen that by properly stimulating them it is possible to prevent and cure various psychosomatic diseases. Stress, anxiety, unexpressed feelings such as anger and sadness accumulate in some specific areas of the body inducing morbid states. Chromotherapy exploits the stimulating and soothing qualities of the range of colors of the chromatic spectrum - the same as the iris, or the rainbow - to bring the chakras, and therefore the entire body, back into balance. Naturally, one cannot think of recovering from serious pathologies solely and exclusively using colors, but without a doubt many ailments can be alleviated, not to mention that associating chromotherapy, which has no side effects, with traditional pharmacological treatments, is useful for enhancing its effects and to relieve the psyche.

Colors can be absorbed by our body in different ways:

- through light irradiations made with special equipment and filters;
- through foods, ie by eating foods with their natural color;
- through sunlight since this light contains all colors in its spectrum;
- through solarised water, i.e. irradiated with a luminous radiation of a precise color which charges it with that energy;
- through clothes,

- through the bathroom, then with waters colored with natural essences or special lights;
- through meditation, following precise techniques;
- through visualization and breathing;
- through massage with special products and colored pigments.

Extroverts choose cool colors like blue, blue, purple, to balance their energy.
Introverts choose warm colors, such as red, orange, yellow. Light is one of the regulatory agents of serotonin, a hormone that regulates mood and all body activities in general. So much so that depressed people are advised to spend more time outdoors, in the sunlight. Chromotherapy is considered a "gentle" non-invasive healing method, which can give benefits and is suitable for everyone, as it does not present particular contraindications. It can be used individually to treat energy imbalances of various kinds, but also as an effective support for other energy treatments and natural therapies.
The main ways of using color therapy are:

- The green light bath, for example, is used for relaxation therapies. The choice of the type of radiation to be used in the color bath must take into account the general situation within which the disharmony manifests itself.
- Total irradiation, in which, through special equipment, several areas of the skin are irradiated at the same time, using lights of different colors.
- Irradiation on a specific area, in which the intervention is focused on the area of energy imbalance. It is essential to identify the exact problem in order to irradiate with appropriate lights.
- Through foods, i.e. by eating foods of one color rather than another, eliminating red colored foods for example, in favor of green ones, as happens in Ayurveda, where the diet prescribed on the basis of the various pathologies also refers to the color of the food.

- Through the clothes you wear, thus favoring a specific color in correspondence with a specific Chakra that you want to stimulate.
- Through meditation, following visualization techniques that involve the use of colors.
- Through massage with special products and colored pigments.
- Irradiations according to acupuncture points: colored light is used instead of needles. It is used to reinforce the missing energy.
- Solarization of water. Solarized water is obtained by placing it in perfectly transparent glass containers, which are irradiated with colored light. The water thus treated is then used for compresses, gargles or as a drink.

In recent years, the design of hospital structures has been oriented towards a chromatic revolution: the cold and aseptic white is replaced by more lively and colorful hues, capable of significantly improving the attitude and condition of patients and helping to create more welcoming and pleasant environments.

In fact, humanization processes and the use of color in healthcare facilities can alleviate the sense of discomfort and instability of patients, helping them recover a more positive and optimistic attitude. The traditional image of the hospital is disappearing to be replaced by a network of social and health structures that respond to a new concept of health, understood no longer as the absence of disease but as a search for well-being. There are various pilot projects based on the criterion of humanization, both as an organizational principle of the service and as a prerequisite for the design of spaces with respect for the person and his emotional condition. The San Bortolo hospital in Vicenza uses colors as a psychological aid to healing, thus becoming the leader of a national project in collaboration with the Milan Polytechnic to make Italian hospitals more human, welcoming and "in colour". The environments are designed according to fluid paths, so that the user has multiple points of view from the room in which he is located towards the other rooms and also towards the outside of the building, rigid, geometric spaces with orthogonal furnishings are eliminated, giving way to soft lines that combine to give the environments fluidity and dynamism. The use of color is fundamental in the humanization of spaces. Indeed, it has been proven that color can change mood, but not only that: being hospitalized in a room with a "positive" color can influence the progress of healing.

- White is depressing, the favorite colors are shades of blue and light blue in all possible shades and green, colors considered more restful, while yellow and orange help to face the day in a more positive way.
- Yellows, oranges and reds would, in particular, have the effect of giving patients a certain energy, helping them to face the day with greater energy, while the softer colors would be much more suitable for meditation, rest and sleep .
- The forest environment is for color experts the model to follow to make an environment more pleasant, with even sudden changes in the chromatic intensities of light and shadows, which break up the monotony of hospital white and neon lighting.

Another interesting project for the humanization of hospital environments is that of the Niguarda Hospital, the work of Jorrit Tornquist, in Milan. Inside this building, the colors help to orientate and better define the spaces to obtain a pleasant environment for both patients and staff.

- The patient rooms are green and orange to lift the spirits, transmit positive sensations of openness to the world and fight withdrawal into oneself.
- For operating theatres, the choice has been oriented towards green colors tending towards blue to reduce the perception of the red complement of blood.
- An orange shade was preferred for the personnel changing rooms, so as to convey energy, industriousness and vitality.

- The gynecology department, on the other hand, has pastel pink tones which inspire feelings of affection and protection, while the corridors are brighter green and pink.
- For the entire structure Tornquist bans the use of red, because it would help to arouse a sense of anxiety and danger, and of blue, which intensifies physical pain.
- In pediatric hospitals, the use of the chromatic language has even more interesting and effective implications for the assistance and care of children: in fact, colors allow young patients to interface positively with the environment that surrounds them, promoting more relaxed and cooperative. In this way the children are able to orient themselves better in a new environment such as the hospital and to experience it with less hostility and greater confidence in themselves and in the doctors. At the new Meyer pediatric hospital in Florence there has been a real chromatic revision of the staff uniforms: the gowns are multi-colored and very colourful, with polka dots and stripes, designed by the children themselves in order to foster the relationship with the doctors and convey a atmosphere of serenity and harmony. The new Meyer also boasts a careful chromatic design of spaces and environments: the white and aseptic corridors are replaced with colored paths and each floor is tinged with a different shade to facilitate orientation within the structure. However, the colors are not limited to spaces and environments but are also used in the details of the furnishings and furniture, highlighting the utmost chromatic care dedicated to the world of children.
- On the ground floor is the Emergency Room with green tones.
- On the first floor, the operating and resuscitation rooms are painted blue.
- The top floor, dedicated to patient rooms, features warm orange tones.

The use of color is also particularly effective for Alzheimer's patients, helping to make spaces more welcoming and recognizable and helping patients to settle in better. Thanks to the use of intense colors, the environments are defined and identified more immediately, helping the patient to achieve a sense of tranquility and emotional and psychological stability. The language of colors becomes a very useful communication tool and prefers strong contrasts of shades, because the nuances are hardly perceived by elderly patients, being careful not to create chromatic combinations that could cause states of stress and anxiety. The "Massimo Lagostina" Alzheimer Center in Omegna is an example of where colors help create pleasant environments, capable of arousing memories and emotions in patients. In this context, an excellent combination is achieved between functionality and the patients' needs for orientation and definition of spaces.

Within this structure, simple rules are observed for an effective chromatic design: the choice of saturated colours, the use of uniform and compact colors for the floors, the ability to communicate the functions and intended uses of the rooms through different shades . In this way patients can move and experience these spaces with more awareness and freedom. In many countries chromotherapy enjoys an excellent reputation and is also used for animals such as, for example, in New Zealand where livestock diseases are treated with wire spirals inserted into the ground and on which different depending on the disease.

The colors therefore have the following effects:

- They dilate or narrow blood vessels.
- They raise or lower blood pressure.
- Increase the production of red blood cells.
- Support white blood cells.
- Destroy bacteria.
- They support the immune system.
- Protect fabrics from aggressors.
- Increase tissue activity.
- They increase the transport of oxygen in the blood.

- They regulate the exchange between tissues and bones.
- Promote the formation of enzymes, trace elements and vitamins.
- They activate and stabilize the metabolism.
- They extend consciousness.

Light irradiation chromotherapy consists in the use of the energy of electromagnetic waves of light which, within a precise wavelength, penetrates the tissues creating the conditions for interacting with the cells, restoring the electrical and chemical balance of the cellular homeostasis by improving its biological functions.

Even this chromotherapy does not cure the symptoms but goes down to the roots of the imbalance and does not leave, like some drugs, harmful residues that the body has to eliminate with difficulty. We should not be surprised by the fact that colored radiation acts on our emotional states, on the trend of our psychic state and on our body, thus promoting balance and physical well-being. Precisely for these reasons, more and more researchers and doctors are focusing on the study of chromotherapy and more and more people are obtaining concrete and visible benefits. Irradiations with colored light beams are therefore able to stimulate the formation of body cells and have an effect on nerves and organs.

As far as the techniques for working with this type of chromotherapy are concerned, we can include:

1. Classic chromotherapy: it consists in irradiating with a specific color and for a certain period of time the areas of the body affected by the disturbance or those reflected.
2. Chromopuncture: it consists in concentrating the radiation on the energy points of the body, i.e. the most receptive ones, meridians and chakras.
3. Color and light bath: it consists of irradiating the whole body with a specific color and for a certain period of time in order to determine complete cell regeneration.
4. Chromatic water bath: it consists of performing a real bath with water that is irradiated with a specific color, and

therefore charged with a precise energy, for a certain period of time.

5. Solarized water: it consists in irradiating natural water, placed on a white glass container, for a certain period with a specific color and then drinking it;

6. Energized foods or clothes: irradiating foods or cloths with a specific color for a certain period of time for eating or wearing them respectively.

Both those who want to preserve psycho-physical balance and those who want to associate the use of light and colors with therapies already in progress can turn to chromotherapy. In fact, chromotherapy is a catalyst for stimulating the body's natural self-healing processes. More often than not, color therapy is an effective healing method for depression, neurosis and anxiety, ailments for which yellow, green and blue colors are used. The most important chromatic benefits are reflected in the chromopuncture for children, aimed at treating hyperactivity, headaches, insomnia and emotional disorders.

The Theory of Color

Light, which contains all wavelengths of visible radiation, generally appears white; entering the eye it creates a visual sensation. Visible radiation is part of the electromagnetic wave field. The radiations visible to the human eye are included in a very limited range of the spectrum between the wavelengths of approximately 380 and 780 nm (nm = nanometres). One nanometer is one billionth of a metre.

In reality this interval is not fixed, since it depends on the sensitivity of the human eye and therefore from subject to subject. This "subjective" aspect is essential for understanding color, each of us has, in fact, the ability to perceive colors in a different way. Man's ability to perceive only such a limited part of electromagnetic radiation in the form of light is due to the particular nature of the human eye. Our eye has the ability to distinguish the different colors, that is, to establish a comparison between waves of different lengths of the visible spectrum. When the eye receives a radiation whose wavelength is, for example, 470 nm, a blue light is perceived, while a radiation of 600 nm corresponds to an orange light. The human eye can only perceive radiation between 4,000 and 8,000 Å (angstroms). Each wavelength band corresponds to a color and has a specific therapeutic action:

• Red: 6200 Å (angstroms) = (620 nanometers)
• Orange: 5890 Å (angstroms) = (589 nanometers)
• Yellow: 5510 Å (angstroms) = (551 nanometers)
• Green: 5120 Å (angstroms) = (512 nanometers)
• Blue: 4750 Å (angstroms) = (475 nanometers)
• Indigo: 4490 Å (angstroms) = (449 nanometers)
• Purple: 4230 Å (angstroms) = (423 nanometers)

Å= (angstrom) unit of measurement of radiation, corresponds to 1/100,000 of a millimetre.

Below the violet we find the ultraviolet and above the red the infrared. The amount of energy of each color is inversely proportional to the wavelength. The higher the wavelength, the stronger the skin penetration and the lower the energy charge.

- So, red is the most penetrating color, then there will be orange, yellow, green, blue, indigo and violet.

The latter reaches limited depths, but infuses a high amount of energy. When all wavelengths of the visible spectrum strike the eye at the same time, white light originates. It is clear that white light is not identified at a certain wavelength but is the result of the fusion of the various colored lights that make up the visible spectrum. A simple demonstration can be done by passing a white light beam through a glass prism; based on the principle of refraction (deflection) of light, from the opposite side of the prism the light will split into different colors. The study of light has brought knowledge of the effect light has on man.

The different wavelengths are interpreted by the brain as colors, ranging from red of the longest wavelengths (lowest frequency), to violet of the shortest wavelengths (highest frequency). Light and colors can help us discover many aspects of our interiority. Color surrounds and permeates everything visible and also not visible to our gaze. The color of the skin shows precise signals in relation to our physical and emotional health. The light and colors of the house in which we live and of the place where we work, determine in a very important way our state of well-being or malaise and our energy in facing everyday life. The therapeutic effect of color on the human organism is linked to the oscillatory nature of our cells: in fact, malaise or disease are nothing more than a disharmony of the cellular vibratory rhythm on which colors have a harmonizing power (the frequencies of the colors interact with the vibrations of our body, rebalancing them in the case of illnesses or ailments).

From a therapeutic point of view (treatment of disorders relating to our body), chromotherapy is considered a "gentle therapy" as it is non-invasive, generally does not present particular side effects and immediately provides a beneficial effect to those who undergo treatment, without creating addiction.

With few exceptions, chromotherapy can be useful for everyone, even on a preventive level. In fact, there are particular treatments that serve to give the individual "tuning", in order to make oneself stronger and prepared to face daily discomforts. Chromotherapy can be applied alone or as an enhancement to other treatments, being a formidable "catalyst" for stimulating natural self-healing processes. People who suffer physically or psychologically can profitably associate chromotherapy with any treatment (allopathic, homeopathic, physiotherapy, reflexology) because it stimulates the natural disposal of toxins mobilized by the active ingredients of the products, cleaning and protecting the whole organism.

Each application can be seen on its own, therefore, even once in a while it can provide a good benefit, but obviously the best results are obtained with a series of sessions: first weekly, then monthly, finally you have the typical "recalls" to seasonal changes. Color is an aspect of visual perception and its evaluation takes place in a completely subjective way. It is therefore necessary a characterization that allows to identify the color and classify it.

Only through an in-depth study of color theory can one understand how its perception works.

Color can be characterized by three main parameters:

1. Hue, tint or chromaticity (Hue) - It is a parameter that identifies the dominant wavelength in the range of the electromagnetic spectrum in the visible. The hue indicates and identifies the color of an object (red, yellow, blue, etc.) also for its denomination.

2. Purity, saturation or fullness (Chroma) - It is the element that expresses the intensity of a colour. A pure color is represented by a monochromatic wavelength. The same color can be obtained with different lights (phenomenon of metamerism), but in this case its saturation can vary.

3. Luminance, clarity or brilliance (Value) - Expresses the luminous intensity in the direction of vision, quantifies how much white or black is present in the perceived colour. The possibility of objectifying a color has always been a complex problem, not yet fully resolved. Color,

being an individual sensation, is actually not measurable. A "standardization" of color is necessary to classify, identify and measure it. From the "physiology of the eye", we know how the photoreceptors of the retina react to light stimuli, in particular how these are equipped with pigments corresponding to red, green and blue.

When the retinal receptors are stimulated in pairs, yellow, cyan and magenta are perceived. The other colors, including orange, gray and brown, are the result of partial stimulation of the receptors.

But how are the different combinations of colors actually defined? First of all, it is necessary to distinguish between two types of mixtures: between colored substances and between colored light rays. The systems that describe how color mixing occurs are:

- Additive color synthesis, which takes place by summation of colored light beams, such as for example for lighting systems or monitors.
- Subtractive color synthesis, which involves the combination of colored pigments, such as for paint colors or for printing processes.
- In general, most of the colors can be obtained by mixing, only three colors cannot be obtained in this way: for the additive synthesis red, green and blue; for subtractive magenta, yellow and cyan.

Colors are divided into three basic categories: Primary Colors, Secondary Colors and Tertiary Colors.

- **Primary colors**

Primary colors are divided into additive primary colors and subtractive primary colors.
Additive primary colors are those colors which when mixed together give rise to white, and are: red, green and blue.

They cannot be generated from other colors.

The three main colors that we are able to perceive are red, green and blue (RGB - Red, Green, Blue). These three colors are conceptually represented by additive color synthesis. When Newton decomposed white light through a prism, he identified the seven main colors resulting from refraction: red, orange, yellow, green, blue, indigo and violet.

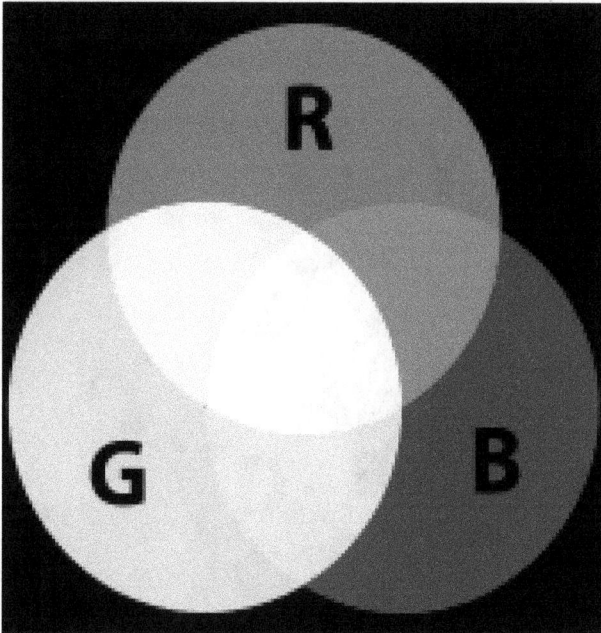

The spectrum of visible light shows three bands of predominant colors: red (R), green (G), and blue (B), the additive primary colors. If we superimpose three beams of light of these three colors (RGB) we obtain white light (W).

The superimposition of two colored lights produces cyan (C), magenta (M) and yellow (Y), the subtractive primary colours.

The RGB model was described in 1931 by the CIE (Commission Internationale de l'Éclairage). The sum of the three main wavelengths, red, green and blue, gives rise to all the other colors. It is necessary to specify that colors such as black, brown and gray are the result of a decrease in brightness in the colour.

The RGB system is used a lot in lighting. The image on the screens is based on light radiation and is formed by additive synthesis. In fact, thanks to this principle, the cathode ray tube of televisions and the color definition of monitors and projectors work.

The subtractive primary colors are those that when mixed together give rise to black and are: yellow, magenta and cyan.

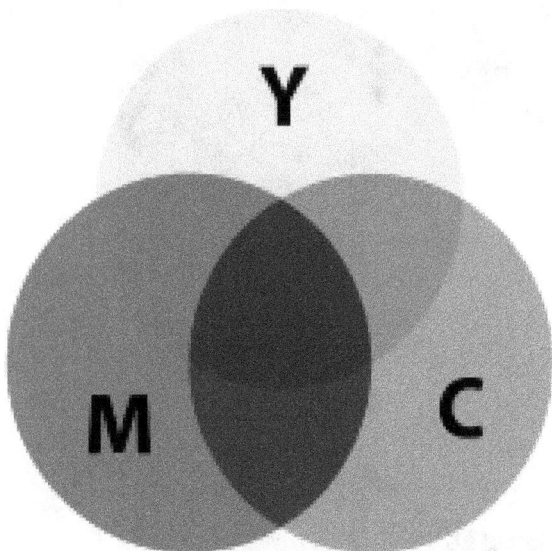

The synthesis or subtractive mixing of colors is based on the removal of the primary colors that make up the white light which is obtained by mixing 100% of the three primary colors (RGB) together. In the subtractive synthesis three basic colors are used from which the others originate: cyan, magenta and yellow (CMY - Cyan, Magenta, Yellow) which are considered the primary subtractive colours. Each of these colors has the property of blocking, i.e. removing from view, one of the primary colors of additive synthesis and reflecting the other two.

- If we remove the red additive primary color, cyan is created. If we perceive the color cyan, the object absorbs the red color and reflects the green and blue.
- Removing the primary color green creates magenta. If we perceive the color magenta, the observed object absorbs green and reflects blue and red
- By removing the blue you get the yellow. So when our eye perceives the color yellow, the observed object absorbs the blue and reflects the green and red.

If each of the primary colors of the subtractive synthesis has the power to absorb a third different color of visible radiation, by mixing all three, the entire visible spectrum will be absorbed and no light will be reflected back to the observer.

The CMY model is the basis of all printing systems, color photography and painting in general. The four-color printing method is the most common, also referred to as the CMYK system (Cyan, Magenta, Yellow, Key black). CMYK uses the three primary colors CMY plus black (K), which has the function of balancing the various shades of colors and giving relief to the image.

- The sum of the three subtractive primary colors, cyan, magenta and yellow, results in black.
- By mixing the three subtractive primary colors (yellow, magenta, cyan), also called fundamental or derivatives, infinite colors can be obtained.

The colors that can be obtained through the four-colour process are the result of a subset of the visible color range, consequently not all the colors we see can be reproduced with this technique.
The same goes for the RGB system which does not have all corresponding colors in the CMY system.

- **Secondary Colors**

Secondary colors are obtained by mixing primary colors two by two.

27

If we mix the CMYK Subtractive Primary Colors, we get:
- yellow + cyan = green
- magenta + cyan = blue
- yellow + magenta = red.

If we mix the RGB Additive primary colors we get:
- red + green = yellow
- red + blue = purple
- blue + green = cyan.

- **Tertiary colors**

Tertiary colors are obtained by mixing two primary colors in different quantities.

For example, mixing red and yellow produces an orange tending more towards red or yellow, depending on whether the quantity of the first or second is greater. Tertiary colors can also be obtained by mixing equal parts of a secondary with a primary.

For example, by adding orange to yellow, you can get a yellow-orange.

In addition to tertiary colors, there are also quaternary colors (equal parts mixing of a primary with a tertiary) and quinary colors (equal parts mixing of a secondary with a tertiary). In the set of primary and secondary colors we have three pairs of colors called complementary.

Complementary colors are pairs of colors, one complementary to the other.

Pairs are formed by a primary and a secondary; the secondary color is the result of the combination between two primaries, the third missing primary is the complement of the secondary:

- Purple is complementary to yellow, because it is the result of the combination of magenta and cyan, the missing primary color, yellow, is the complement of purple and vice versa.
- Green is complementary to red. Magenta and green are complementary, because only yellow and cyan are used to make green, and there is not even a bit of magenta. The

color green, located in the center of the light spectrum, represents the point of balance between all the chromatic categories and develops a stabilizing force and general well-being.
- Orange is complementary to blue.

Johannes Itten, color theorist, in 1961 created a chromatic circle demonstrating how all other colors could be derived from primary colors. Itten's circle helps in understanding the chromatic combinations between primary, secondary, tertiary and complementary and serves to understand the chromatic contrasts.

In the center of the circle is a triangle containing the three primary colors, which are red, yellow and blue. From the mixing of these colors we obtain the secondary colors around the triangle to form a hexagon, and they are green, orange and purple. Finally, it can be seen that the circle is closed with 12 colors which are primary, secondary and tertiary, i.e. the other colors that are obtained from further mixing. The colors positioned diametrically opposite each other are the complementary ones (yellow and purple, red and green, blue and orange).

- Black and white represent two "particular colors", also defined as "non-colors". In terms of additive color synthesis, black is the absence of light, therefore the absence of color, while white is the sum of all the colors of light; vice versa for the subtractive synthesis black is the result of the sum of all the colors, while white is the absence of color. Surfaces that completely absorb light, instead of reflecting it, return black.

Therefore, black and white vary their compositional characteristics according to the starting conceptual model, whether additive or subtractive. An object that reflects all light waves appears white (white = sum of all colors); the object capable of absorbing all the waves, without returning them to our eyes, is black (black = absence of colours); a surface that absorbs all but one visible radiation has the color corresponding to that single wave (for example: an object that does not absorb green is seen by our eyes as green).

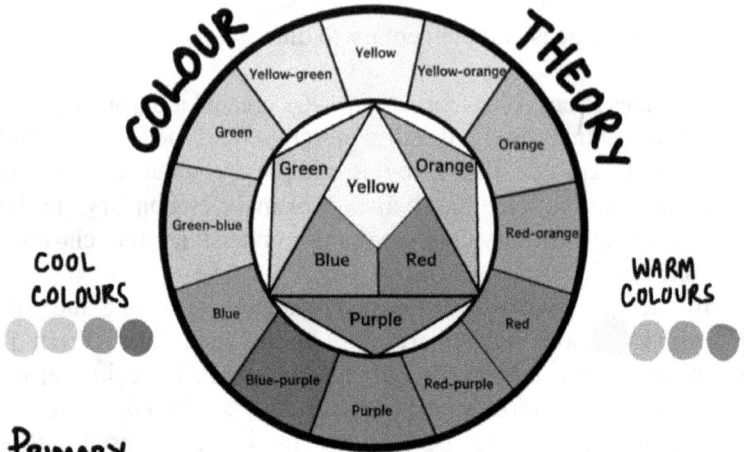

COLOUR THEORY

Yellow
Yellow-green · Yellow-orange
Green
Green · Orange
Yellow
Orange
Green-blue
Red-orange
Blue · Red
Blue
Purple
Red
Blue-purple · Red-purple
Purple

COOL COLOURS

WARM COLOURS

PRIMARY

Mixing different amounts of the primary colours can make all the colours of the colour wheel.

Yellow · Blue · Red

SECONDARY

Mixing two primary colours make a secondary colour

Orange · Green · Purple

TERTIARY

Primary colours and secondary colours mixed together.

Blue-purple · Red-orange · Yellow-green

Green-blue · Red-purple · Yellow-orange

COMPLEMENTARY

Colours opposite from each other on the colour wheel.

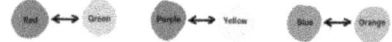

Red ←→ Green   Purple ←→ Yellow   Blue ←→ Orange

ANALOGOUS

Colours that are neighbours on the wheel.

MONOCHROMATIC

A colour with its tints and shades. Tints are colours mixed with white. Shades are colours mixed with black.

Colors can also be divided according to the sensation they communicate, distinguishing them into warm and cold colors.

In general, reds, yellows and oranges are associated with sunlight and its heat, therefore classified as warm, while blues, purples and greens, recalling snow, ice, sea and sky, are defined as cold . In reality, this distinction is not always valid, because depending on the color combinations, even a cold color can be perceived as warm and vice versa.

- Warm shades: those that tend towards orange and red. These colors enhance muscle activity, blood pressure, breathing frequency and heart rate. In general, these colors can be traced back to tone and action.
- Cool tones: those that tend towards purple and blue. These colors tend to have a calming, purifying, relaxing effect and are used to lower blood pressure, heart rate and respiratory parameters.
- Neutral shades: those tending towards black, white and grey.

The function of colors in food

Foods have different colors and different functions and beneficial properties can be linked to them: for this reason it is called the "rainbow diet". In fact, foods can be divided into seven different groups, all marked by a different color: red, orange, yellow, green, black, blue and white foods.

- **Red foods**

Eating red helps to regain self-confidence, to ward off melancholy and depression as bright red vegetables have a stimulating effect. With foods of this colour, tomatoes, strawberries, cherries, watermelon, we fill up on youth: they contain antioxidant substances and lycopene, a carotene which helps prevent gastrointestinal tumours. The purplish-red hue in fruits and berries is due to the storm and improves the immune system. Bright red foods should be eaten in the first part of the day: tomatoes, strawberries, radishes. From noon to midnight, however, the red fades, goes out and therefore the foods to prefer are: red beets, red grapes, legumes, plums. Rich in "fire", red foods are a charge of powerful energy for the whole body. Take plenty of it if you feel tired, fatigued, lethargic and lacking strength. Excellent stimulants, they reactivate the metabolism and thus help to lose a few pounds in view of the departure for the summer holidays. The only warning, do not abuse it if you are hypertensive or choleric.

- **Orange foods**

Orange at the table stimulates the appetite, physical and mental synergy. Eating orange helps to listen to yourself, to understand your real needs, your emotions. It is advisable to eat intense orange foods such as apricots, melons, citrus fruits, pumpkin, peaches from midnight to noon; on the contrary, from noon to midnight it is better to prefer carrots, tangerines, star anise, herbal teas.

- **Yellow foods**

Eating yellow means stimulating good mood, concentration and creativity. At noon the sun reaches its maximum expression therefore it is advisable to eat intense yellow foods until the first part of the day. In the second part, however, you can consume foods with a colder yellow color such as pineapple, papaya, yellow beans, Belgian endive. Yellow-orange foods, lemons, grapefruit, oranges, peppers, carrots, apricots, peaches, strengthen the immune system. It has long been known that yellow-orange vegetables have a tonic effect on mood. In addition, they are rich in beta-carotene, which carries out a protective action against free radicals, protecting cells from aging. Yellow-orange foods have a good anti-stress effect. Consume them often in times of high tension and overwork.

- **Green foods**

Green, like orange, is a "middle" color between blue and yellow. It is the color of nature, of relaxation, of calm.
Eating green helps to give serenity, to support the nervous system, to feel at peace with the world. The color of green vegetables is given by chlorophyll, which is rich in magnesium and helps regulate the metabolism of fats and sugars. Lighter foods tending towards white, garlic, leeks, onions, are rich in allyl sulphide, a substance that lowers blood pressure and cholesterol. Green is a balancing colour, and due to this characteristic it should not be missing from any meal. It is particularly recommended for anxious people, when stress gives rise to headaches or gastritis. As usual, intense green foods should be eaten in the first part of the day: avocado, cucumber, lettuce, rocket, olives. From midday to midnight, algae, asparagus, green beans are better.

- **Black foods**

Black is the color of fertility. It has a strong erotic value despite being considered the color that absorbs energy. In Nature, in fact, many seeds, a symbol of life, are black in colour, just think of the seeds of pears, pumpkins and sunflowers. In its various nuances we can find foods ranging from black/purple, black/blue to black/indigo: aubergines, figs, plums, seaweed, black corn, blackberries, black olives, potatoes. The blue of myrtillin, especially present in berries, improves the transmission of nerve impulses.

The purple of rutin and quercetin, present in many fruits and vegetables, has a revitalizing effect, promotes tissue oxygenation and has a protective action on the capillaries. Black foods are consumed in the evening as they promote sleep and are very digestible. Conversely, black foods with red-brown hues such as tea and coffee should be consumed in the first part of the day due to their energizing properties.

- **Blue foods**

Blue is relaxing and helps restore optimal psychophysical balance. Choose foods of this shade if you need to regain calm or if you suffer from insomnia. Aubergines, figs, black grapes, plums, berries, blueberries, belonging to the Blue/Purple class, protect against cardiovascular pathologies and, thanks to anthocyanins, improve the structure of the capillaries by reactivating the microcirculation, as well as stimulating urinary function. blue-violet group, currants and radicchio are excellent antioxidants because they are rich in vitamin C and protagonists in the formation of carnitine and collagen. Furthermore, radicchio, like figs, currants, blackberries and plums, contains potassium which protects bone tissue and decreases the risk of cardiovascular diseases and hypertension. Magnesium is rich in eggplants which are, on the other hand, low in calories. Berries, on the other hand, cure capillary fragility and prevent urinary tract infections, are friends of a healthy intestine with their soluble fiber which regulates the absorption of other nutrients and feeds the intestinal microbial flora. Again: in the blue-violet there are foods rich in fiber and carotenoids, active against tumors, cardiovascular diseases including stroke, cataracts, cellular aging, neurodegenerative diseases and skin aging.

- **White foods**

White symbolizes peace, honesty and intelligence, gives clarity. It is the color of simplicity and purification, therefore it brings us back to basic foods such as milk, carbohydrates in general, in grains, flakes, flour or semolina, better still if wholemeal. It is advisable to eat white foods in the first part of the day. Eating white prepares us for tranquility and balance to face daily challenges not only in the social but also in the private sphere.

To make the most of these properties, it is good to consume foods according to a precise pattern:
- Yellow, orange and red foods in the morning, for full energy: citrus juices, raspberries, apples, melons, apricots, peaches.
- At lunch, green, yellow and white foods: green salads and vegetables, with broad strokes of yellow. A brightly colored minestrone is also perfect.
- Blue and black colors are recommended for dinner: radicchio, purplish-red cabbage, plums, "black" grapes, aubergines, beets, figs, dates and wild berries.

Chromotherapy with water

Each color has particular and unique effects on living organisms. According to Theo Gimbel, one of the most important figures in the field of modern chromotherapy, colour, having a much faster vibration than sound, exerts a much more powerful and profound influence on the human organism than that of sound waves. In fact, it has been shown that, in the presence of color, biochemical changes occur within cells throughout the body, due to the action of hormones that are released into the blood, the production of which is influenced by the perception of colors.

The method of chromotherapy with water therefore consists in "impregnating" the molecular or vibrational structure of the water (or of another liquid) with the specific vibrations of light of a colour, so as to be able to fully assimilate them both by drinking them and by applying them to the body.

Direct sunlight acts as a powerful activator, transferring color vibrations to the water in a process that is referred to as "solarisation" or magnetization. It is one of the most ancient chromotherapy techniques, used since time immemorial in India, and it is also one of the simplest, most delicate and safest.

First, use purified or spring water. Put it in a bottle or other transparent glass container, cover it with a cloth or sheet of paper of the chosen colour, then expose it to direct sunlight. In summer, an hour of exposure to midday light may be enough (or two or three in early morning sun), while in winter it will be necessary to leave it for a few hours. The longer the water is left in the sun, the greater its power will be.

Leave it, then, to cool and drink it during the day.

- Solarized waters should be taken in variable doses, from a spoon to a glass, twenty minutes before the three main meals.
- In acute cases, the administration can also be carried out every half hour, in the average dose of half a glass.
- In chronic cases, the administration can be extended even for several months.

36

If you store it in the refrigerator, it will keep its effects for at least three days. Solarized water should always be sipped. Do not expose water to neon or fluorescent light as it has a filtered, ineffective light frequency. Use cork stoppers, which is a natural material, avoiding plastic and metal stoppers.

To increase its beneficial effect, it can be associated with flower therapy (Bach flowers), adding 10-12 drops of the essential oil suitable for the purpose:

- Red solarized water: aspen, beech, crab apple, elm, mustard, olive, willow.
- Orange solarized water: agrimony, aspen, cerato, cherry plum, chicory, clematis, holly, honeysuckle, pine, willow.
- Yellow solarized water: beech, centaury, heather, hornbem, impatiens, mimulus, wild oat, wild rose.
- Blue solarized water: chestnut bud, gorse, oak, rock rose.
- Green solarized water: centaury, cerato, impatiens, red chestnut, sclerantus, vervain, vine, water violet.
- Indigo solarized water: cerato, gentian, gorse, hornbem, larch, sclerantus, walnut, white chestnut.
- Purple solarized water: rock water, star of bethlehem, walnut, willow.

It should be remembered that solarised water with colors at the extreme red of the solar spectrum (red, orange, yellow) should not be taken in the evening before going to bed, because it causes insomnia, unlike that impregnated with blue or violet, which it should be drunk before going to bed to resolve this disorder. Furthermore, the latter slightly modifies the taste, making you perceive sweeter foods, while red water gives foods a slightly bitter taste. It is also possible to use honey instead of water. In this case, it must be left exposed to light (solar and lunar) for three days and three nights. Honey retains the properties of the colors much longer than water, if you are however careful to always store it in a cool and dark place.

Just take a teaspoon a day. Solarized water can also be used effectively by adding it to the tub when you take a bath.

- Red solarized water

It is anti-inflammatory and can be indicated to all those who have emotional overloads and strengthens the immune system. It is stimulating, energizing, warming, exciting and helps to reactivate blood circulation. It is energetic for the liver and has a beneficial action on the muscular structure. Stimulates, excites and accelerates the pulse, raises blood pressure, stimulates the muscles and reproductive organs. It can be useful in case of physical weakness, frigidity, impotence, hypotension, hypothyroidism, sore throat, slow metabolism, dry skin, colds. It is contraindicated in the presence of fever, acute inflammation, hypertension, anxiety, agitation and insomnia.

- Wrinkles and stretch marks: treat the affected areas with red solarised water.
- Sunburns: immediately apply compresses, to be repeated several times, with red solarised water.

The red solarized water keeps for up to two days, it must be used only when our nervous system is not agitated, when we don't have inflammation in progress and we don't suffer from insomnia. It is used in the morning in the measure of a spoon or two, then before the main meals; in the evening it is not recommended for those who find it difficult to sleep.
In acute problems you can take half a glass of solar water a day, but if we go to work on some of our chronic ailments we will use it for longer periods but only 3-4 tablespoons a day.

- Orange solarized water

Facilitates intestinal rebalancing, strengthens the immune system, tones and helps to fight depressive states. It is indicated against water retention in the legs and promotes the functionality of the pancreas and spleen. Its ingestion brings physical and mental energy into harmony, helping to achieve a state of well-being and joy.

- Yellow solarized water

Rebalances the intestine, tones the nervous system and helps in overloading the respiratory system. It has a reinforcing action for motor activities. It is an anti depressant par excellence. It has a stimulating effect on mood, promotes learning, and improves communication skills and interpersonal relationships. It is indicated for anorexic people, who have digestive problems, liver problems, abdominal swelling, intoxications, drowsiness, cellulite. It is not suitable for those with acute inflammation, neuralgia, heart palpitations and dysentery.

- Green solarized water

Helps fight headaches due to stressful situations. The green color refreshes, calms and relaxes both physically and mentally, facilitating sleep. It is the color of youth, fertility and new life. It is the color of self-preservation and nature. It is a symbol of balance and stability. It has no contraindications.

- Blue solarized water

It has antibacterial and bactericidal properties; this color contributes to the dissolution of all states of anxiety and related emotions, asthmatic and respiratory problems with related imbalances, repressed emotions, cramps, infections, joint pain, cardiac overloads. In addition to being extremely healthy, this water helps to rework the negative mechanisms that our subconscious continues to implement constantly and automatically, eliminates emotional blocks and wounds, brings negative thoughts to the surface to then be eliminated through sweating or urine.
As it relaxes you can drink a nice sip of blue solar water before meditation to reach a deeper level or before going to bed for a relaxed sleep. You can drink blue water whenever you want.
- Eczema, skin inflammations in general: compresses of blue solarised water several times a day.

- Burns from thermal sources: immediately apply compresses, to be repeated several times, with blue solarised water.
- Conjunctivitis: blue solarized water to be used as eye drops, 1-2 drops per eye.

It is the color of emotional serenity and relaxation. For some traditions it symbolizes divine wisdom. It is not suitable for people prone to depression. Since blue has an antiseptic action and prevents water from becoming infected, water stored in a container of this color retains its properties from one week to ten days, both at high and low temperatures.

- Indigo solarized water

To recover from psychosomatic diseases, such as psoriasis, eczema, urticaria, it is recommended to drink water kept in bottles of this color. Being rebalancing it is indicated for hyper emotional people. It also helps to purify the body of toxins and enhances muscle tone, sight, hearing and smell. On a psychic level it is indicated for emotional people, hypochondriacs, or who have obsessions, hallucinations or who are affected by senile dementia.

- Violet solarized water

This color helps fight bacterial and viral diseases, invites calm, tranquility, promotes sleep and a meditative state. It also helps fight nervousness and irritability. The purple color favors inspiration and spirituality. On an emotional level it helps mentally fatigued people who have suffered trauma or are subject to nervous excitement. Do not use in case of sadness and depression or on distracted people as it would increase the loss of the sense of reality.

Red

Red is the first color of the rainbow and it is also believed to be the first color perceived by children, the first to which all peoples have given a name. Red, of all colors, is considered the color par excellence and is opposed to black and white, considered in their sense of light and darkness and with which, in the Middle Ages, it formed a symbolic triad. The importance of the color red dates back to the early days of humanity when man painted the walls in caves with black and ocher figures.

The red color symbol, like all symbols, has both positive and negative values. On the one hand, red is the color of love, both earthly and spiritual, just think of the Sacred Heart of Jesus, of passion, of activity, of emotions, of sentiment, of expansiveness, of liveliness, of blood understood as life , on the other it is the color of anger, violence, aggression, bloodshed.

- In Ancient Egypt it had a positive meaning only when it indicated the red crown of Lower Egypt. Red was put in direct relation with the evil Seth and with the equally evil god Apophis, the snake. In the papyri their names were generally written in red and red animals, such as some types of dogs then common in Egypt, were kept away from the community because their color was associated with aggression and violence.
- In the pre-Columbian art of ancient Mexico, red was used very rarely and generally in relation to blood, the sun, fire and the representation of the liver. Among the Mayans it was considered the representation of the East, while among the highlanders of ancient Mexico, red represented the South.
- In ancient China, red was the sacred and vital color of the Chou dynasty. Red was also the color of the god of happiness who dispenses wealth to men. In Europe the combination of red-green complements is considered harsh and aggressive while in China it expressed vitality in relation. Red-haired men were considered in China

husbands severely tested by married life and destined for an early death.

- In traditional Christian art, red was the color of the sacrificial blood of Christ and the Martyrs, of fervent love (red was the garment of John, beloved among the apostles), and of the Pentecostal flame of the Holy Spirit. The red of the cardinals' robes indicated that whoever wore this robe should always be ready to shed their blood for the defense of the Church. In sacred vestments red is the color worn in the celebration of martyrs, the Holy Spirit, and the Passion.

Red has been called "the great energetic activator", the "father of vitality" because of its immense elemental effect on the physical structure of man. This color has a "very warm" energy. It is the color with the greatest penetration characteristics of the visible spectrum. Red represents a physiological condition of stimulus and excitement, its effects on the body are: it acts on the heart by increasing the number of beats and, therefore, blood circulation, raises blood pressure, increases the respiratory rate, stimulates nervous activity and glandular, acts as a stimulating element for the secretion of cerebrospinal fluid, activates the liver, sensory nerves and all the senses. It is also beneficial for the muscular system and for the left cerebral hemisphere. The red rays break down the salt crystals in the body and act as a catalyst for the ionization process, without which nothing could be absorbed into the body. These ions are the conductors of electromagnetic energy in the body. The red color breaks down crystals composed of iron and salt into iron and salt, with the result that the iron is absorbed by the red blood cells, while the salt is eliminated through the kidneys and skin. From a psychological point of view, the color red symbolizes health, fire, hot blood, anger, choleric temper, danger, destruction.

• It has a stimulating and exciting function.
• Provides man with a feeling of power.
• Red is used to bring the extrovert back into their shell.

The color red is associated with the 1st chakra.

The first chakra is called the base chakra or root chakra and is, therefore, connected with earthly existence on a purely physical level and with the sense of smell. It is the first of the seven energy centers of our body and is located at the base of the spine, in the perineum area, between the genitals and the anus. It is the first Chakra starting from the bottom and this position makes it the support of all the others. Its symbol is the red lotus with four petals inscribed in gold with the last four consonants of the Sanskrit alphabet: «v, sh (lingual), sh (palatal), s».

Muladhara is a single vortex pointing downwards towards the earth, it has no front or back movement like the other chakras. From here originate the three energy channels Sushumna, Ida and Pingala. Its functioning harmonizes with the seventh chakra, therefore with the hypothalamic-pituitary-gonad-adrenal neuro-hormonal axis. Through this energy center the knowledge stored in the collective unconscious manifests itself.

The Muladhara chakra constitutes the foundation and root of the chakra energy system, as through it the energy emanating from the earth and nature is collected and subsequently transformed. It is, therefore, the foundation of the other chakras, it is the earth in which to anchor the roots and give stability, security and defense. Its main function is survival and the associated keyword: I exist. It is oriented vertically with the funnel opening towards the Earth. Its main function would be linked to the material body, to the survival instinct and would produce a sense of physical and mental harmony in relation to nature, satisfying primordial needs such as food, water, air, rest. Since it only has one pole, it would tend to be a bit larger than the other chakras. Its geometric symbol is the triangle with a vertex at the bottom enclosed in a square, the first emblems of the female sexual organ and the second of the Earth element; in it sleeps Kundalini.

An "earth energy" would arrive from this chakra and its closing would produce the sensation that "the earth is missing under your feet". In Greek mythology it is said that man was created from clay and that our mother is Gea, the Earth. The first chakra indicates how the person is at that moment with respect to his physical energies. If the person is happy to live, if he is in good health, at least if he believes he has a good relationship with his body, if he wants to have fun, to play. This Chakra is normally associated with the adrenal glands, lower limbs, spine, large intestine, genitals, and central nervous system. It develops from the moment of birth to the completion of the first 24 months of life, allowing the child to grow physically and to develop motor skills. The Root Chakra has a strong influence on one's career and relationship with money. Its proper functioning affects professional life, financial balance and one's sense of belonging.

If there is excessive functioning of this Chakra, both thoughts and actions will be oriented towards the obsessive satisfaction of material needs and personal safety; you will want to possess everything you want, while it will be difficult to give or donate anything. If hindered, one reacts with aggression, anger, violence, feelings or methods that express a defensive attitude, linked to the lack of trust in the ancestral vital forces; in this attitude there is always the fear of losing what gives security and a sense of well-being.

If, on the other hand, there is insufficient functionality, there will be weakness and poor physical and emotional resistance. Many things will be lived with excessive concern, even if they are very trivial. Existential insecurity, in the meaning most linked to primordial instincts, will be the main problem, you will feel as if you have lost all footholds. Every fact of life will become insurmountable, therefore easier, more pleasant and less tiring conditions will be dreamed of, generating mental escapes from contingent reality. If the upper Chakras have developed more than the lower ones, one will have the sensation of being out of touch with the world, deeply experiencing a sense of estrangement and absolute and hopeless loneliness.

If the energy block also affects the third Chakra, in addition to the first, one could find oneself in the presence of anorexia.

The pathologies that can cause its disharmonious functioning are due to:

- Physical complaints, such as bowel disease, constipation, hemorrhoids, sciatic nerve disorders, back pain, varicose veins, bladder and kidney disorders, prostate pain, bone disease, anemia, blood pressure fluctuations.

- Mental disorders, such as phobias, weakness, depression, lack of confidence, tendency to depend too much on others.

The sense of the first chakra is smell, the first sense that the newborn actively uses. Animals are recognized primarily through smell; they know how to recognize the smell of fear (the adrenaline that escapes from the pores when we "sweat cold"). This is why dogs know who is afraid. Adrenaline causes blood vessels to constrict, thereby increasing blood pressure. The effect is twofold: a greater quantity of blood nourishes the muscles but blocks the digestive functions. The use of perfumes indicates that smell is an important sense. However, those who are in good health and who follow the right diet do not need deodorants or perfumes, because they will already have a pleasant and attractive smell. Smell receptors are located at the base of the brain and feed directly into the limbic system, which is the area of memory and emotion. Therefore, aromas can immediately access emotional memories that are found in our unconscious. The animal of the first chakra is the elephant with seven trunks. In Europe too, the elephant suggests primordial strength: it knows how to stay in a group and knows how to die alone. We appreciate this animal's intellect because it remembers its benefactors (as well as its enemies) and is gentle: it only eats vegetables and knows its own strength, it will never crush a living being. The representation with seven trunks seems curious: it symbolizes the seven aspects of life as a whole and of each specific period, the seven types of energy that are available during the day, in short, the seven chakras. Each chakra supplies prana to a different endocrine gland. Just as there are seven chakras, there are seven endocrine glands.

Both the chakras and the endocrine glands are located along the spinal column. The endocrine glands produce hormones and supply them to the bloodstream. These glands lack an excretory duct, so the hormones are released directly into the bloodstream where they are carried to every organ and tissue by the blood to exert their influence on all functions of the physical body. Each gland is internally related to other glands and also works closely with the nervous and circulatory systems.

For the body's organs to work efficiently, the blood must contain certain chemicals and these chemicals are secreted by the endocrine glands. The secretion of the glands into the endocrine system is vital to the health of the entire system. Our bodies can get sick if there are too few or too many hormones. The endocrine glands of the first chakra are the adrenal glands. There are two adrenal glands located above the top of each of the two kidneys. The adrenal glands are the body's call to battle. When adrenaline is released into the system, our perceptions become clearer, we have new vigor and feel more courageous. The release of adrenaline activates the fight/flight syndrome, which prepares us for battle or flight.

The release of adrenaline and the activation of fight/flight are generated by real or imagined dangers. Thus, our emotions can trigger an adrenaline release when we feel extreme fear or even chronic anxiety. The first chakra is the "survival chakra" and the fight/flight syndrome is vital to the survival of the species. According to the doctrine of Yoga, the energy of the Kundalini (sexual energy) resides in this chakra: if the base is stable, the energy can ascend through the other chakras thus accelerating the development of the personality. As mentioned, the First Chakra is the main generator of the human energy system and is connected with all solid things that exist on earth, primarily the body and the satisfaction of essential needs. The subjects focused in Muladhara are very strong and resistant people, endowed with a concrete temperament, oriented towards the simple satisfaction of material needs. They have a slow and limited mind, but effective for everything related to the relationship with material objects or the ability to survive and the task of obtaining the necessary.

They usually choose jobs that require a lot of muscle strength, or related to the production of solid and resistant objects, or repetitive jobs. In cases where the Chakra is fairly balanced, they also reveal themselves to be very constant people, with very little imagination and a great attachment to traditions, family habits and place of birth.

- Chakra in a state of lightness: it is the enlightened condition of the Chakra, in which the capacities for concreteness that are typical of this center are placed at the service of an idea and a purpose. Subjects with an almost infinite patience. It also develops a proper attention to the body and its health.

- Chakra in a dynamic state: it is marked by a great energy which is applied in work and in the production of objects, in building and in accumulating material goods. Instinct for hunting and fighting. If there is a strong excess of Rajas, it will give rise to action aimed at accumulation, difficulties in relationships due to excessive attachment and pettiness, dispersive and meaningless acting, highly destructive impulses.
- Chakra in a state of heaviness: heaviness is the quality of the energy that naturally dominates this Chakra. If a further excess of Tamas develops, a state of inertia, dullness, laziness, drowsiness, brutality and unconsciousness is created. Nutrition, aerobic movement, regular practice of Asana and Pranayama and positive mental stimuli are the best way out of this dangerous and obscure condition, which can block evolution and push the individual towards very low and degenerates.

The metals that radiate red rays are: iron, rubidium, titanium, bismuth, zinc, copper (the latter also radiates its complementary color, green).
One caution: If you use too much red or too often, it can cause fever and exhaustion; mostly red should therefore be used in combination with blue.

- Those who prefer red want to win and long for positions of power. He is a person with great energy who loves to act and always put himself in competition with others and, above all, with himself. He has a bold character and always wants to catch the attention of others. The major defects of those who prefer this color are presumption, irascibility and restlessness. If the red color is excessive, the person will therefore be aggressive, presumptuous, irascible, restless, quarrelsome, argumentative, will tend

47

to always talk, will not give space to other people's speeches and will always want to be right.

- Those who shun the color Red are restless people, often unable to face the difficulties that life presents them. Almost always in the background, he prefers to keep the others going, thus remaining behind the scenes without the desire to be a protagonist. Predominantly stable in daily choices, he often tends to take well-trodden and safe paths instead of attempting an adventure by taking other paths. He hates the expansiveness of others, thus taking refuge in his perennial introversion. If the red color is at fault, the person will therefore tend to be introverted, shy to the point of being fearful, will have difficulty facing the hardships and challenges of life, will tend to stay aloof, will prefer to be the gray eminence who holds the power behind the scenes. He will not like novelty, surprises, adventure, risk, he will often be intransigent with others and with himself.

Furnishing-wise, red exudes warmth and is suitable for north-facing rooms, however, it should not be chosen to paint the walls, as the spaces seem smaller. Instead, it is recommended for details such as cushions, curtains, throws, sofa coverings, tablecloths, vases, lamps, and gives a special touch to any environment. However, scientific studies have shown that being surrounded by red walls leads to an increase in heart rate, causes an increase in vital functions, increases aggression and energy. Red is the ideal color for those who want warmth, intensity and vitality at home. Have fun with its multiple shades, but dose this color carefully; you can choose, for example, a frame, a vase, a cushion or other accessories. Rich, bright tones lend a dramatic edge, so large areas in red are suitable for dramatic effect. A red light makes the room warm and welcoming. Red is inspiring and brightens up any room. However, if you are reluctant to use strong tones of red, you could choose the natural tones of terracotta and wood, which allow you to make elegant combinations without using too bright colors. Even red accessories are ideal for those who don't dare to choose this color for large surfaces. If you don't choose red because it seems too bold and difficult to match, remember that in nature, red tones never seem intrusive. Inspire yourself by the red of gardens, hedges, woods, you will discover flashy but not out of tune shades. Depending on the atmosphere you want to create, red can be combined with colors that accentuate or attenuate its warm and stimulating effect. Once the shades have been chosen, nothing prevents you from mixing a red or light pink with turquoise, orange and yellow, to give an exotic touch to a large room. As a primary color, red is very refined when combined with e.g. with navy blue and fir green. Terracotta or light pinks combined with jeans blue and olive green are also very elegant. Red and gold are the traditional colors of a luxurious setting, even better if by candlelight. Red and white always give an impression of purity and freshness; white softens the aggressiveness of red.

Red is contraindicated in the following cases:
- Individuals with red hair
- Hypertension
- People with emotional disorders
- Excitable temperaments

Insanity - The use of red in most mental and emotional disorders should be avoided, except for catatonic patients, i.e. those who persist in any bodily attitude.

Therapeutic use of the color red :
- Presbyopia - Red is useful for individuals suffering from presbyopia as it leads the individual to become self-centered. Red, in this case, pushes the individual into himself; in fact, the farsighted is too open to the outside and is not self-centered enough.
- Coccygeal plexus area - Red rays stimulate this area, causing the multiplication of hemoglobin and red blood cells; they also control body temperature and act on the endocrine system through this area.

49

- Stimulates the release of adrenaline and slightly raises blood pressure.
- Anemia - Promotes circulation, for example if irradiated on the soles of the feet; it increases the number of red blood cells and is therefore useful in case of anemia.

- Physical wasting.
- Circulatory problems - Exposure to red has been shown to accelerate heartbeats.
- Diseases of the endocrine system - In this case red plays an important role. In addition to fighting stress, it performs a vital function for human health, physically, mentally, emotionally and spiritually.
- Partial and total paralysis.
- Depressive states - It is very useful in case of melancholy and depression, because it makes you talkative, open, thoughtful and passionate.
- Red is beneficial for the muscular system and the left cerebral hemisphere.
- Influenza states (only in case of fever).

Orange

In chromotherapy, orange represents the color of those who need optimism, instinct and the pleasure of the senses; orange gives joy and frees from the grip of depression, transforming the environment. The color orange is a symbol of inner harmony, of artistic and sexual creativity, of self-confidence and in others.
As a warm color, orange promotes blood circulation, releasing tensions especially those that lurk along the back.

- It is the result of the combination of red and yellow rays; being halfway between these two colors, it has a warming, cheering and energetic action, but not as exciting as red nor as electric as yellow.

The choice of orange indicates the need to search for intense experiences, in every aspect, from which to draw and experience new pleasant and cognitive sensations. Red is physical strength-love and yellow wisdom-knowledge; united in orange they express this combination of characteristics. The orange color comes from ancient cultures, ancient religions and remote symbols. The name "orange" or "orange" has Arabic origins, and recalls the name of gold.

- In oriental culture, the color orange is associated with properties that favor mental concentration. For this reason, Buddhist monks wear a habit of this color, which has the purpose of facilitating the detachment from earthly and carnal passions.
- In Chinese, the word "orange" has the same sound as "pray for good luck." In China, in fact, the color orange is considered a propitiator of good luck.

In chromotherapy, orange helps to assimilate negative feelings and to deal with the traumatic events of existence such as the loss of a loved one or the end of a relationship.
Furthermore, it is indicated when you feel stuck, at a standstill in your life and are afraid to face the changes necessary to leave

the past behind and look to the future. The action associated with this color is expansion, understood as opening to life.

Orange is the color of the 2nd chakra.

The second chakra is called the sacral chakra, center of the cross. Its symbol is the orange lotus with six petals; the letters Bam, Bham, Mam, Yam, Ram and Lam of the Sanskrit alphabet are inscribed on these petals. It is located in the lower abdomen, just above the pubis, in correspondence with the sacrum (three fingers below the navel near the sacral plexus). The second is the chakra of the continuation of the species and, therefore, of reproduction and as a logical consequence it is the source of energy and sexual pleasure. Its symbol is the upward-facing crescent moon. The key word is "I feel", the bodily feeling of sensations, whether pleasant or unpleasant. It develops from about the seventh year of age until about the fourteenth. In women it turns clockwise, in men counterclockwise. The second chakra is associated with the emotional body, the water element, taste (tongue) and action (hands). The glands controlled by it are the gonads (ovaries and testicles). Its function is linked to desire, pleasure, sexuality, procreation, the ability to experience non-mental primordial emotions. The organs connected with the second Chakra are: intestine, bladder, uterus, ovaries, prostate. The kidneys are just the symbol of fear. The dysfunctions of the second Chakra cause impotence, frigidity, pathologies of the genital system, also at the lesion level (fibromas, prostate adenomas), of the urinary system and lumbosacral stiffness.

From a psychological point of view, a decompensated second Chakra leads to lack of self-esteem, phobias, panic and anxiety. From an emotional point of view, the imbalance of this Chakra can lead to the obsessive search for pleasure, also and above all on a sexual level up to aberration, if it is hyperfunctioning, but also to a total closure towards the sexuality of life, generating a sort of anesthesia of the ability to experience non-intellectual joy, if it is instead hypofunctional.

This Chakra is often found decompensated in female subjects (it should be remembered that the proper polarity of this Chakra, like that of all even Chakras, is Yin). The second Chakra indicates our emotional part, our fears, the things that have scared us, that paralyze us. It is the first step of energy towards dematerialization. It is always worth remembering that the four alchemical principles are basically the four principles of energy:

- 1st principle: in one is all, that is, in my cell the same thing happens that happens in the cell of the galaxy.
- 2nd principle: matter is the invisible part of the invisible, i.e. what we see materialized, is the part that we have made tangible with respect to the homologous invisible energy.
- 3rd principle: as above so below and vice versa, i.e. Yin and Yang, black and white, day and night, light and dark, i.e. what happens on one level also happens on the other other level.
- 4th principle: nature is constantly renewed by fire, that is to say that only in faith what burns inside you allows you to renew your life.

By acting on the second chakra, what is commonly referred to as a self-healing process occurs. Once balanced, its positive energy will expand to all other chakras accordingly. It is therefore a very important chakra (as indeed are the others), whose correct activity allows the human being to appreciate life and, therefore, make it easier and more pleasant in a certain sense - and not only with the half of the sky – or on the contrary, in case of incorrect flow, transform it into a small but very efficient personal hell that ends up reflecting also on those who are nearby: wife, husband, partner, children, parents.

The effects of orange on the body: it has a strong stimulating action on the thyroid gland; it is antispasmodic (excellent for contractures and muscle cramps); does not increase blood pressure but stimulates the heart rate and the expansion capacity of the lungs; optimizes the activity of the spleen.

In chromotherapy, orange is often used to replace red when one wants to avoid overly vigorous stimulation.

- People who prefer Orange show a clear vitality and energy: the preference for this color therefore makes these people capable of extraordinary enterprises; undertakings, however, always serene and thoughtful. Anyone who loves Orange is also a person who tends to be optimistic and aware of their own abilities, placing boundless trust in themselves without any presumption. He loves with joy and transport and is generally in perfect harmony with everything around him. The wearer expresses joy and self-affirmation, good humor and altruism.

- Those who reject Orange tend to constantly control their emotions. He often finds it difficult to relate to others and, if there is a problem, he is led to exaggerate it, thus believing he is unable to solve it. Those who shun the color Orange usually do not weigh decisions and act on impulse: this way of dealing with situations, which at first may seem effective for achieving great goals, is blocked by the tendency to pessimism inherent in those who do not like this color . He also finds a lot of difficulty both in the sexual and sentimental spheres, never abandoning himself completely with confidence, but delegating any type of move to reason.

The balanced characteristics, in orange, are: graceful movements, emotional intelligence (right side of the brain), knowing how to experience pleasure, knowing how to take care of oneself and others, ability to change.

- A strong lack of orange can indicate: rigidity of the body, frigidity, limited social practices, denial of pleasure, excessive defenses, fear of changes, lack of desire, lack of passion.
- An excessive presence of orange, can indicate: exhibitionism, obsession with pleasure, being dominated by emotions, experiencing emotions in an excessive way (hysteria, destructive crises), emotionality, excessive sensitivity, obsessive attachment, emotional dependence, invasion of others in its own sphere.

Remember that the electromagnetic energy of orange is on the same vibrational frequency as the DNA chain. A meaning of nourishment and energy has been recognized to the color Orange. In fact, it can influence the problems caused by anxiety with a physiological effect of environmental and physical satisfaction.

The presence of this color is able to modify the anxious person on a psychological level because its action reverberates on the emotions that are the basis of affective disorders, from which all the disturbances that arise in the sphere of anxiety, generic or phobic, originate , or associated with panic attacks, compulsions and obsessions.

Indications:
- With crystals you can have a double action that combines color with the power of the stones: therefore orange agate, stone of the sun, fire opal.
- Has a softer effect than red, so it stimulates the heart without affecting blood pressure.
- Stimulates the appetite for which it is an anti-anorexic.
- It is useful in case of apathy, depression, pessimism, fear, neurosis, psychosis.
- By helping to remove deposits from bones, it can provide relief for those suffering from severe rheumatism.
- Relieves cramps and relieves muscle tension and contractures.

Contraindications:
- Inflammations.
- Liver disease.
- Bleeding.

Yellow

For chromotherapy, but not only, yellow represents a vital color that underlines the search for the new. Here this power that distinguishes yellow in chromotherapy is used in various circumstances of psychophysical discomfort, apathy and depression. Yellow seems to be even more effective in situations of eating disorder, in cases of inappetence and chronic anorexia, as the specific chromatic vibrations are able to stimulate the metabolism and the sense of hunger. The use of yellow stimulates rationality and the left side of the brain, also improving gastric functions and toning the lymphatic system. Helps eliminate toxins through the liver and intestines. In ancient Egypt this color was associated with the God of the Sun, who represented strength and vitality. In China, however, it was a color associated with the spirituality and sacredness of the Buddha.

- Yellow brings relaxation where there is tension in the muscles due to nervousness, tension, fear, anxiety.
- Indicated for people who feel lack of involvement, desire for control and deep insecurity. Stimulates mental activity and brings confidence and security by giving joy.
- Being a stimulating colour, it should be avoided in cases of hysteria and acute inflammatory states (colitis, gastritis).
- Effects on the psyche: constituent of the nervous system, it is a strong stimulator of cheerfulness, sense of well-being, extroversion and conscious lucidity.

It is a "hot" type of energy.
Yellow is lighter than red and, therefore, more suggestive than stimulating, so its impulse acts in flashes.
Yellow is the color of emotional detachment and as such, it also helps us to take work matters more lightly, easing the stress load.

- Those who prefer the color yellow are extroverts who welcome new things with joy and are usually endowed with a fervent imagination. Those who prefer the yellow color show a vitality in alternating phases with more or less high peaks. Very prolific in terms of ideas that he applies to the real world, he is also subject to rapid changes in front. He has many expectations about his future and loves renewing himself and making new experiences. He often tends to seek the approval of the people around him and does everything possible for him to be admired. He also suffers from loneliness.

- Those who shun the color yellow often feel disappointed in their expectations and little esteemed by the people who are part of their circle of acquaintances. He often falls into the trap of little trust in his means even if this gap can be filled even if only by accumulating lost energy.

Yellow is the color of the 3rd chakra.

The third chakra is called the solar plexus chakra, or navel chakra. In Sanskrit it is called Manipura, which means city of jewels. Its symbol is a yellow lotus flower with ten petals, on which are the letters Dam, Dham, Nam, Tam, Tham, Dam, Dham, Nam, Pam, Pham. At the center of the flower are the red triangle of Fire (Tejas), the syllable/root "Ram" and a ram, the traditional messenger of Agni, the Hindu Lord of Fire. It is located in the solar plexus/dome of the diaphragm.

From a psycho-energetic point of view, its most important function is related to personal affirmation and the exercise of individual power with respect to society and the environment in general; it indicates the realization of the person, how feasible the person sees his desire for life, how much a person wants and wishes to fight for himself, how much a person loves himself.

It develops from 4/6 years until the end of childhood, around 10/12 years, allowing the boy / girl to gain their independence and achieve emotional separation from their parents.

The main pathologies expressed by the third Chakra concern all metabolic diseases, such as diabetes, hyperlipidemia, liver failure, cirrhosis, gastric and duodenal ulcers, glycemic levels, as well as all pathologies concerning the processes of nutrition, digestion and assimilation . From the psycho-energetic point of view it is at the level of this Chakra that the emotional forces directed towards the external environment are generated: feelings of friendship, resentment, sympathy, antipathy. The third chakra, in particular, is the expression of the awareness that everyone has of themselves: that ability to feel pleasure in knowing that they are satisfied, but also the humility that distinguishes those who know they can always improve, because growth lies in change.

It is the Chakra of individual will, charisma and efficiency; it is the foundation of social personality.

Its excessive functioning causes inability to remain calm, outbursts of anger, hyperactivity, upset stomach of nervous origin; poor functioning instead causes low energy, shyness, continuous need to resort to stimulants or stimulants. The disharmonious functioning of this Chakra generates the unbridled desire for power, for manipulation, to be able to distort reality always and in one's favour; you will tend to notice a hyperactive attitude, which is implemented to hide the sense of inadequacy and emptiness that is caused by the impotence to manage situations of absolute power that one would claim to exercise. Inner serenity will be greatly compromised and, obviously, the satisfaction of material well-being will be the main one, albeit at the expense of any pleasant feeling, even going so far as to consider them undesirable and annoying. The subject who suffers from a decompensation of the third Chakra is led to lose control of his own emotions and to develop a highly aggressive attitude, necessary in order not to allow others to bare his own inner weakness, a fact which would unmask the power games of in which this subject lives, creating a situation of energetic paralysis which would express itself as desperate and despairing impotence. An example of this defeated subject can be given by the image of those people who are generally middle-aged, but increasingly also young, who spend their time in annihilating and destructive activities, such as drinking, using

58

drugs more or less recognized as such, and who generally have a highly aggressive and prevaricating attitude in the family. These, in fact, are followed by a highly depressive situation. In this case the subject will have the main objective of being accepted and well-liked by others, and to achieve this goal he will deny himself in order to conform to the way of thinking of the people he wishes to like, suffocating and completely denying his own desires and emotions; nevertheless, indeed, precisely because of this frustrating attitude, bullying and harassment towards members of one's family will increase. Powerful and solar Chakra, it reveals to everyone their right to exist and their place in the Universe, promoting self-acceptance. Through its totally harmonious expression, the human being is in the world with the fullness of his physical and mental attributes and allows him to act on the material level in a loose and harmonious way, promoting the enjoyment of everything.

If the third chakra is not perfectly harmonious it can fuel one's sense of inferiority; they can decrease one's real mental abilities, such as logic and rationality, and therefore increase confusion and a sense of insecurity. It can happen that one's desire for power, possession and, consequently, also for oppression of others is fueled in order to obtain and excel. Will and power represent for everyone, in current society (especially Western), one of the keys to success, but they can represent, when understood in an egoic sense of possession and hoarding, the impossibility of conscious access to the other chakras and, therefore, to a real fullness of one's Being.

It would be related to the stomach, intestines, liver, gallbladder, spleen, pancreas. It would stop due to great frights (with contraction of the stomach) or as a reaction to situations or people that are not accepted and this blockage would cause inability to remain calm, outbursts of anger, hyperactivity, disturbances of nervous origin. The element of this chakra is fire. The sense organ related to the manipura are the eyes, seat of sight, while the organ of action is the anus, i.e. the excretory apparatus (however also connected with muladhara) which conveys the waste produced by the process of transformation and assimilation that fire performs. The main feature of this chakra is heat, so the concentration on it favors heating and combustion. The choice of yellow is therefore a search for the new, for change, for liberation from the schemes. Synonymous with liveliness, extroversion, lightness, growth and change.

• Whoever wears yellow feels good about himself; it is, in fact, the color associated with the sense of identity, with the ego, with extroversion. Always denotes a strong personality, dominant, intellectual, courageous, responsible, insecure, coordinated, sociable and friendly.

It is contraindicated in all situations of excessive nervousness and irritability, acute palpitations and dysentery. Yellow foods, such as lemons, grapefruit, oranges, peppers, melons, pineapples, yellow plums, bananas, vegetable oils are the richest in vitamin C which strengthens the immune system and has a purifying effect on the whole body. They also contain two antioxidants, zeaxanthin and lutein, which strengthen eyesight. And then, carotene in abundance, essential for protecting cells from aging. Yellow is cheerful, it lifts your spirits and brings joy to any environment. It is the lightest color on the color scale and has a revitalizing effect on any room, even in the purest and most intense shades. Yellow fills the house with sunshine regardless of the tones you have chosen: warm like saffron, sunflower, ocher or cold like lemon, primrose or butter yellow. Yellow is the ideal color if you want a room full of light and sunshine: even cold colors like greens and blues become warmer, and neutral colors more interesting. It is no coincidence that lemon yellow and ocher prevail in Provence. Some shades of yellow feel warm and shimmer like gold. But there are also cooler tones like primrose yellow. A flamboyant lemon yellow, especially when combined with bright green and light turquoise, communicates energy. Rooms with little light acquire warmth and freshness. Yellow brings warm accents to rather cold environments and enhances details, but it can also be used on larger surfaces due to its light and bright tones suitable for rooms of all sizes and all light conditions. Yellow increases the attractiveness of sunny rooms and gives warmth and light to colder ones facing north; for this reason yellow is often used, when natural light is scarce. Blue and yellow are a very cheerful combination, conjuring joyful visions of sea and sand, sunflowers and summer sky. An intense egg yellow is a strong color and requires strong combinations. It's gorgeous with navy blue and fresh leafy green. Blue-grey, mint green and baby blue go best with primrose yellow and buttercream. Yellow should be used in meeting and conference rooms and classrooms, to promote better communication. It is also suitable in the dining room or living room due to its natural vitality, capable of creating a comfortable and welcoming atmosphere.

Indications:
- Bronchitis
- Spleen - exerts an inhibitory function on the spleen, acts as a purgative, regulates bile flow, fights parasites.
- Aesthetics: it is mainly used in case of oily, asphyxiated, acneic skin and in lymphatic stasis. Its action is restructuring, bio-revitalizing and above all antioxidant.
- With yellow the functioning of the cells improves and the skin gains in elasticity, freshness and beauty.
- Nervous breakdown
- Intoxications of the skin - The irradiation of yellow facilitates the disappearance of scars, even from acne.
- Poor concentration - Increases efficiency, amplifies communication and expressive skills, encourages concentration and clarity of reasoning, stimulates memory and thinking skills. Writing on light yellow paper helps clarify ideas if they are confused.
- Rheumatism
- Sinusitis
- Constipation

Contraindications:
- Delirium and hysteria
- Gastritis with muscle spasm
- Feverish and inflammatory states.

Green

Green in chromotherapy plays a fundamental role, as green is harmony. It is the color of nature and of the balance between the forces in play. It is the color of the drive towards well-being, towards green fields, towards calm and refreshment. This is also given by the fact that green represents a neutral color with respect to the fulcrum of the solar spectrum, therefore it is the right color for balance. Green is therefore the color with which to paint calm and serenity. This is perhaps the reason why Indian culture uses this color for the earth, associating it with the positive vibrations of our thoughts and our senses. Yes, because green does not heat or cool, it is neither acid nor alkaline. Green is the color of nature, it is a symbol of renewal, balance, hope, development and fertility. It is the therapeutic color par excellence. Energy of the "neutral" type, neither hot nor cold, has powerful rebalancing properties. In the light spectrum, green is located in the center between cold and warm colors: it represents their synthesis and therefore performs a function of balance.

- From a physiological point of view it promotes the general well-being of the organism, increases its vitality and restores the balance of its functions.
- It is used for the treatment of stress, anxiety, hyperactivity, headache and some forms of insomnia.
- It is also effective in bulimia and in all psychosomatic forms that affect the gastrointestinal tract (gastroduodenal ulcer).
- It is also a powerful germicide and antibacterial.
- Positively affects asthma, cough, joint inflammation, burns, bronchial diseases and the like.
- Detoxifies and decongests the body.

It is the color of concentration and guarantees precise control, exact analysis, coherent logic, good ability to record and remember.

The desire for green meadows and trees that one feels after a period spent among the gray pebbles and red bricks of the cities represents the instinctive yearning for the invigorating color of nature, which gives calm and refreshment; green is the neutral color with respect to the fulcrum of the solar spectrum, the balancing point.

- Those who prefer the color green tend to exalt themselves, often giving the feeling of feeling superior to others. Furthermore, those who love the color green are characterized by the continuous desire to make a good impression and impress; he does not accept changes in his ways of acting since, feeling himself the best, adapting to others would demean him in his high self-esteem. Conservative and habitual, those who choose green often feel insecure, demonstrating fragility towards themselves.

- Those who refuse green are constantly suffocated by the grip of obligations and feel compelled to take actions and do what they don't want. He often gets frustrated because he believes that she doesn't live up to her high expectations of him.

Green is the color of the 4th chakra.

The fourth chakra is also called the heart chakra, the heart center. Its symbol is the twelve-petalled green lotus on which the twelve Sanskrit letters stand out k, kh, g, gh, n (guttural), c, ch, j, jh, n (palatal), t, th (lingual), and is located in the region between the heart and the two nipples. Its geometric symbol is the double crossed triangle (six-pointed star). This chakra is located at the level of the cardiac plexus, behind the sternum, in the axis of the spinal cord and is the center of the entire Chakra system. Due to its position, but also due to its function, it is the Chakra around which all the physical and energetic functions of man "revolve", it constitutes the transition and connection point between the three lower Chakras and the three upper ones. All the other Chakras therefore depend on this, since the heart is considered the seat of the spirit and the center from which all human emotions arise, especially love.

In the Heart Chakra resides the divine spark that is within each of us, here is our enlightened nature, our Higher Self.

This Chakra is considered the gateway to the soul, here feelings such as unconditional love, joy, inner peace, compassion, but also pain and emotional suffering originate. Every form of love originates here, whether it is love towards another person or the unconditional love that binds us to the universe. In it, up to the age of 12, antibodies would be produced, sent into the "subtle system" (a concept of Indian philosophy whose existence has no scientific confirmation, however) against external attacks on the body and psyche. It develops during adolescence, from 12/13 years to the beginning of youth, towards 20/25 years.

Improper development or blockage of the heart chakra would cause feelings of insecurity. This chakra is associated with a healthy and dynamic personality, full of love and compassion and a love of family. It would close in case of conflicts in the family, abandonment, loss of a loved one. This closure would over time affect the heart and lungs and cause pneumonia, asthma, heart disease. The pathologies connected to its imbalance are asthma, arterial hypertension, heart pathologies, pulmonary pathologies. In the case of disharmonious functioning, on a physical level there may be symptoms in the chest, such as a sense of constriction, dyspnoea, arrhythmias, tachycardia, palpitations, asthma and so on, without however having objective evidence from clinical investigations. From a psychic and emotional point of view, we tend to love others only as a function of the acknowledgments and gratitude that they can give in return. If, on the other hand, the Chakra is hypofunctional, on a physical level a malfunction of the diaphragm will be highlighted, with respiratory and cardiac problems, while from a psychic and emotional point of view there will be a tendency to express feelings of hatred and resentment, or of coldness, indifference or insensitivity. It is through the harmonic activity of this Chakra that people are able to sympathize with everything that exists and to grasp its beauty and harmony.

Indeed, the function of this energy center is that of the ability to express pure and unconditional love. The fourth Chakra is the center that allows the development and use of the ability to transform and heal oneself and others. The fourth is the middle chakra, the bridge that transforms and makes compatible the energies of the first three chakras, making them rise upwards, and of the last three, making them descend downwards. It allows you to love in a total sense and without conditions, everything and everyone. When the fourth chakra is open and vital, it makes it possible to relate to reality, seeing its entirety and accepting both its beauty and its negative aspects, enabling the person to give love without expecting anything in return. In his posterior vision he represents the will of his own ego towards the external world, united with the divine will. It favors a harmonious vision of what surrounds the person and enables him to have positive attitudes regarding his own actions, seeing others as support for what he is doing.

- It's also the chakra through which all the energy you want to donate to others passes. Only if the fourth chakra is open and vital can healing energy be given.

When it is closed or not harmonious, the person is hardly able to love and experience others, God or Destiny as you want to call them, in antithesis with themselves, as obstacles to their own fulfilment. And then we risk becoming aggressive and, instead of seeking help from others, we place ourselves in the classic condition of "me against everyone", instantly falling back into the disharmonious energy of the third chakra. Only if you consciously enter the energy of the fourth chakra, carrying and experiencing love and compassion, will you be able to give full meaning to your existence. The opening of the fourth chakra is therefore essential for the therapist: only by working with the heart can he, in fact, be placed in total availability towards others and in total sharing, while maintaining the necessary detachment.

This chakra would also be associated with the thymus gland.

The thymus is a small lymphoid organ located under the breastbone that grows rapidly from birth to two years of age, then undergoes progressive atrophy and its activity is carried out by the immune system. It secretes hormone-like substances that increase the amount of white blood cells. Particularly participates in the maturation process of T lymphocytes.

The position of the thymus, close to the heart and the immune function are elements that signify a defensive role, the creation of a barrier which, if strengthened beyond a certain limit, can prevent love from entering the heart. In the absence of the thymus, the immune capacity does not develop and therefore there is no organic possibility of distinguishing the self from what is other than the self, the attacked from the aggressor. There is no possibility of balancing the opposites, of defending one's individuality. In this sense, the thymus guarantees the establishment of the maintenance of a harmonious balance between inside and outside, thus constituting the center of the individual's existence, its possibility of recognizing itself. The correlated element is air represented by the smoky gray yantra made up of two triangles that intersect forming a six-pointed star, the central symbol of balance.

The sense organ related to the anahata is the skin, seat of touch, while the organ of action are the genitals for the Shritattvacintamani, the hands and the faculty of grasping for some contemporary yoga masters. The main feature of this chakra is mobility, so the concentration operated on the anahata makes what you want move. The bijamantra «yam», i.e. the nasalized letter «ya», is that of the god Pavana, lord of the wind, represented as a smoky gray deity with four arms, the goad in one hand, seated on a black antelope. The heart distributes to the whole body, through the circulatory system, the blood that contains the oxygen fixed in the lungs during inspiration. It is here, like a sun that spreads its energy, a fire that, instead of burning, radiates its heat, warming and spreading life. Oxygen is, moreover, from an alchemical point of view, a solar element: fire can only burn in the presence of oxygen. Carbon dioxide returns to the heart and is released into the environment during expiration. It is thus a complete cycle, marked by the rhythmic repetition of systoles, a centrifugal force that sends blood to the body, and diastoles, a centripetal force that brings blood back to the heart.

Two complementary phases, active and passive, birth (systole) and death (diastole), which repeat themselves continuously, cycle after cycle, and must be in perfect balance for the individual to exist. The cardiac system is completely involuntary. The innervation of the heart, as well as that of the lungs (pulmonary and cardiac plexuses), comes, as far as the sympathetic nerve is concerned, from the band between the third cervical and fifth dorsal vertebra, involving the first, second and third cervical ganglion and the first thoracic ganglia; as regards the parasympathetic, from the vagus nerve that comes from the brainstem. The sympathetic system increases the frequency of the heartbeat and the force of contraction while, on the other hand, the parasympathetic has a function of decelerating the heartbeat. The so high position of the area of origin of these nerves may seem strange but, once again, it is enough to go back to the embryological development to explain this apparent discrepancy. In fact, in the very first stages of embryonic development, during the gastrulation process, a part of the mesoderm migrates up to the front of the pharyngeal membrane and unites with the homologous part of the opposite side (cardiac tube) forming the cardiac sketch, which only subsequently will place in a more ventral position (with the delimitation of the body of the embryo on the 22nd day).

But the innervation will remain linked to the cervical metameres of its initial development. These metamers are also related to arm development. This link explains why arm-related pain can occur in heart-related conditions (for example, angina and heart attack). The lungs, similarly to the digestive system, put the inside in communication with the outside, they are a link between the individual and the cosmos, but for an energy that is more subtle than food, purer. On the other hand, in more ancient stages of phylogeny, the respiratory and digestive functions were undifferentiated: «heavy» elements and «subtle» elements entered the organism together. Even today, the phylogenetically more primitive species (fish) maintain a single duct used both for feeding and for breathing (extroversion in the lateral walls of the digestive tract), while in other animals and in man a separation develops between the two functions : from the pharynx a "bag" differentiates which will become the lung which, therefore, is of common derivation with the digestive. In this case a possibility is evolving to extract a more subtle matter, to separate the light from the heavy. The lung, in fact, captures the prana of the cosmos and "makes" it individual, puts the external "sun" (oxygen) in communication with the internal "sun" (heart).

It is also the respiratory system which scans a complete cycle through each inhalation and exhalation and which, in turn, are centripetal force and centrifugal force, birth and death, passivity and activity, brought together in a perfectly balanced rhythm. But, unlike cardiac activity, respiratory activity is also voluntary, that is, it can be directed, modified, guided by consciousness. It is precisely to this thread (the possibility of voluntary control) that the yogi attaches himself to control, through breathing, the entire organism with its functions that are in themselves far from the domain of consciousness. Therefore, in this wheel there is also the balance of the conscious-unconscious duality, as foreseen by the cycle expressed by the number 12.

Therefore, also in the organs of the anahata chakra we find cycles characterized by complementarity of rhythms and functions which, in their balance, define the individuality of man.

- If this color is in balance it will give calm, equilibrium, serenity, it will make diplomats, persevering, altruistic, sensual, lovers of wealth and beautiful things.
- If green is found in excess we will be disinclined to accept criticism, very demanding, eager for gratification and certainty, prone to fits of anger, possessive, jealous, envious, are brought to excessive sacrifice. An excess of green energy could cause: unconscious fears, biliary dysfunctions, blood pressure alterations, sensation of shortness of breath, reduction of the immune system, propensity for seasonal infections, muscle tension.
- If the color green is at fault, antisocial, intolerant, emotionally cold behavior is assumed, one is inclined to

criticize, to have a melancholy, little empathic, narcissistic character, with difficulty in evaluating and solving problems, afraid of establishing deep relationships, suffocated from family and work obligations. The lack of green energy could cause: marked melancholy, headache, insomnia, indeed, stress, eye fatigue, gastric disorders.

Indications:

- Calming - Promotes self-esteem: therefore excellent for those who are not sure of their abilities and always need the opinion of others. It promotes physical and mental relaxation (it lowers the metabolic rate) and is used in case of stress, anxiety, hyperactivity, insomnia and headaches caused by overwork.
- Intoxications - It is useful for lungs, liver and kidneys when they have to work in conditions of significant pollution, both environmental and food.
- Eye problems - The use of glasses with green lenses tones the optic nerve: by carrying out precision work using a green light, the eyes tire less.
- Effects on the psyche - calms, relaxes, eliminates tension, increases awareness, stimulates the eyes and enhances a good mood. With the green color we obtain a harmony of the body.
- Headaches - It is very useful in case of headaches, neuralgia and fevers.
- Palpitations - Green promotes harmony as it has a calming influence on the nervous system.
- Decongests the body - At the table it is indicated for all those who tend to eat voraciously, as it helps to maintain a slower pace.

Contraindications:

- Depression - Green seems to have no particular contraindications, except in cases of depression, when a more lively color is preferable.
- Asthenia.

Why does green have a relaxing effect on our psyche?

Because the lens of the eye focuses the light of this shade more easily than the others, without any effort; this explains the feeling of peace that this color instills.

But if green is the color of rest, one can also become "green with rage", a way of saying that finds its explanation in the fact that green is a sign of serious illness for the human body.

The green color of vegetables is given by chlorophyll, rich in magnesium, which helps regulate the metabolism of fats and sugars. The list of green foods is long and in spring we have the maximum variety: just think of all the green leafy vegetables and green vegetables and legumes such as peas, broad beans, asparagus, spinach, broccoli, cucumbers, basil, artichokes , parsley, green salad, zucchini: all foods rich in chlorophyll, magnesium, selenium, polyphenols, carotenoids and vitamin C which promote the proper functioning of the vascular system and the conduction of nerve impulses. Magnesium is also of fundamental importance for numerous enzymatic processes that are involved in the absorption of other minerals such as calcium, phosphorus, sodium and potassium: all of which are precious for the health of bones, teeth, eyesight and the cardiovascular system.

Vitamin C and polyphenols, on the other hand, have an anti-tumor action and are blood purifiers, promote lymphatic drainage and are again useful for the heart and blood vessels. As for fruit, thinking green we have kiwis, white grapes, limes, avocados.

Blue

Symbol of harmony and balance, as well as calm, the color blue has the ability to relax, bringing balance to the emotional sphere.
It is a "cold" type of energy.
The "cosmic" color of energy, it represents the intuition that supports the meditative activity. Unlike the color red, it has marked calming properties. Blue is the color of the sky, of the sea, of infinite space and represents, in opposition to yellow, earth-mother, physical, feminine, sky-father, metaphysical, masculine. For Chinese medicine it is a yin color, a symbol of immortality. Due to its high vibration, it has the ability to broaden our understanding and to cure ailments affecting sensory organs such as eyes, nose, ears. It has antiseptic, astringent and anesthetizing properties. It is used in all symptoms that develop heat and pain: sore throat, laryngitis, hoarseness, fever, spasms, rheumatism. In the color scale, blue contrasts with yellow which is the color of the earth and of all that is corporeal. It is however complementary to orange which has similar characteristics because it is "feminine" and metaphysical.

- From a physiological point of view, it stimulates the parasympathetic system, decreases blood pressure, respiratory rhythm and heartbeat, and is therefore indicated for those suffering from high blood pressure, tachycardia and palpitations.
- It also has antispathetic, refreshing, analgesic, relaxing effects.
- It is useful in all cases where there is an inflammatory process: sore throat, hoarseness, toothache, stomatitis but also redness and skin burns, insect bites and skin itching.
- Excellent for sedating acute pain, especially joint pain, and for reducing feverish states.

It fights both physical and mental agitation and is therefore used in psychotherapy to promote relaxation and relaxation. It represents intellect, truth, fidelity, constancy.

Blue is the color of great depth, the feminine principle. It is the color of calm, infinity, peace, emotional serenity and harmony. Unlike the color red, it has marked calming properties. Very useful in case of stress, nervousness, anxiety, insomnia, irritability and inflammation.

- Those who prefer Blue are individuals with deep feelings, calm and with a strong ability to find their inner balance. He is a person who makes ideals his trump card and finds stability thanks to his attachment to traditions. Generally, the person who loves the color Blue tends to avoid particularly chaotic environments and angry people.

- The person who rejects Blue is usually anxious and feels that her qualities are underappreciated. He avoids all the situations that make his life unsatisfying and all the environments in which he doesn't feel in harmony. He tends to get depressed if everything around him is not in keeping with his way of seeing and the lifestyle he has imagined for himself.

In clothing it is a color that extinguishes violent passions and induces a state of calm: this color should be worn to face life's difficult trials. People who wear light blue tend towards introversion and a certain external closure.

It is the color of the phlegmatic temperament.

Blue is the color of the 5th chakra.

The fifth chakra, Vishuddha, the Throat Chakra, is located in the throat at the level of the thyroid gland. It is the center of the human ability to express, communicate and be inspired, creativity understood in a subtle sense, the relationship with our feelings. It is associated with the ability to communicate and express oneself, both verbally and in artistic forms, especially music, dance, acting. The sense connected with the fifth chakra is, not surprisingly, that of hearing.

Indeed, through the ears, we perceive words, music and singing, artistic expressions which, among other things, are particularly therapeutic. The fifth chakra, which connects the lower ones with the crown ones, thus acting as an intermediary between thought and feeling, also represents at the same time the expression of all the chakras: in fact, it is through words, laughter and tears that we give vent to ideas , opinions, sensations of all kinds. The sixteen-petal lotus, symbol of this chakra, contains a yellow circle inside which a white triangle is inscribed, with the point facing downwards. At the bottom of the circle sits a gray elephant. The dominant color of the fifth chakra is a bright blue/azure, a color that induces tranquility. It relates to taste, hearing, smell.

It develops in adulthood and allows the person to express himself (thoughts and emotions), to find his own voice and to listen to others. It allows the individual to resonate with people and places. When the fifth chakra is open and functioning, the human being is aware of the responsibility of his own nourishment in all senses: from the satisfaction of his material needs to the more spiritual ones and he understands, therefore, that he is directly responsible for what he receives and than it assimilates. It is the awareness of one's role in society and in the workplace and one takes action for maximum satisfaction.

If the fifth chakra is not harmonious, fears arise that what one receives from others could be negative (and generally one does not expect positive things) one closes oneself to receiving and assimilating, becoming potentially aggressive in an instinctive defense movement . In its posterior aspect the disharmony of the chakra leads to the fear of failure in social life and work. It leads to the emergence of the victim complex, to hide behind pride, as a defense of real or hypothetical failures and to close contacts with others for fear of being rejected.

It is the chakra of purification and communication which are sound and vibration. Precisely through the deep awareness of this chakra it is possible to open the door of the spiritual path and, therefore, the beginning of contact with the deepest part of oneself, starting precisely with communicating with one's higher self.

The closure of the fifth chakra also creates negative reflections in the external expression (communication) with physical side effects. This chakra would be located at the level of the Adam's apple in men and in the hollow of the throat in women and would be responsible for the functioning of the neck, tongue, neck, mouth, ears, nose, teeth. Through it communication with others and with the deities would take place and it would be the source of the mantras that are sung. On a physiological level, it would control the functioning of the thyroid. With the chakra open, the person would communicate with a clear and firm voice, while it would close when the expression of one's personality is blocked and when there is dissatisfaction with one's work or studies. Closure would cause speechlessness, stiff neck, and throat and thyroid disease.

When developed, it would in fact confer the power to express oneself and speak in an extremely persuasive and convincing way. It's the exchange, giving to receive. In the Throat Chakra, the creativity of the sacral Chakra joins the energies of the other Chakras. We can only express what we have within ourselves, and one of the purposes of the fifth Chakra is precisely to allow us a certain inner space, which allows us to reflect on our thoughts and behaviors. When we develop the Throat Chakra, our thoughts will no longer be dominated by emotions or physical sensations, which therefore makes objective knowledge possible. The physical pathologies related to it refer to the organic or functional diseases related to the organs it governs.

The timbre and tone of the voice are manifestations of the energies of the fifth Chakra: the more harmonious, full and round the voice is, the more this center will be in balance. The psychic pathologies that refer to vishudda all refer to the ability to communicate, not only towards the outside, but also towards one's own interiority; it is through this Chakra that communication between mind and body takes place; therefore the so-called psychosomatic diseases can also - The stones connected with the fifth Chakra are: Sodalite, Lapis Lazuli, Turquoise, Larimar, Blue Tourmaline Indicolite, Chalcedony,

74

Blue Topaz, Celestine, Aquamarine, Chrysocolla, Labradorite, Green Calcite and Blue Calcite.

It is located in the throat and is "pure", as its name suggests, since by now the yogi has purified himself on his journey of ascent and reactivation of the chakras. Vishuddha appears as a purple lotus, according to the Shritattvacintamani, turquoise, according to other more recent schools, with sixteen petals on which the sixteen vowels of the Sanskrit alphabet are represented: a (short), a (long), i (short) , i (long), u (short), u (long), r (considered vowel, short), r (long), l (considered vowel, short), l (long), e, ai, o, au, n (as nasalization), h (as half aspiration).

The related element is ether (also in the sense of space), represented by a circular mandala as white as the full moon. The sense organ related to the vishuddha is the ear, the seat of hearing, while the organ of action is the mouth. The main feature of this chakra is emptiness, so concentration on vishuddha realizes emptiness.

The bijamantra «ham», i.e. the nasalized letter «ha», is that of the ethereal region, represented as a snow-white god with four arms, with the knot and the goad in two hands and the other two dispels fear and in that bestows gifts, sitting on a white elephant.

Exactly at the point where yogis place the chakra there is a very important gland, the thyroid, with four small glands attached, the parathyroids.

Furthermore, in the innermost part of the throat, the vocal cords have the same topographic location, the seat of articulated sounds or of the word and of the capacity for language which is the conscious expression of the concept. The thyroid, of endodermal derivation, develops from the floor of the primitive pharynx whose cells, at a very early stage in the evolution of vertebrates, had acquired the ability to capture the iodine dissolved in the body fluids. The stalk, which connects the thyroid to the floor of the pharynx in the embryo, usually disappears in the adult. In some species of elasmobranchs (class of fish), however, a duct remains that opens into the floor of the pharynx. On several occasions yogis speak of the possibility of "reactivating old energy circuits" and very often in the phylogenetic path one finds "passages", "connections" now lost, but which once had a functional meaning.

Thyroid hormones are of two types: iodine-thyronines and calcitonin. Through iodine-thyronine the thyroid regulates all metabolic processes and energy exchanges, in particular through the metabolism of glycides (sugars). The brain uses almost exclusively carbohydrates for its functions. The thyroid influences body growth and, in particular, brain development, by increasing, for example, the number of synapses, i.e. the connections between nerve cells. It also affects sexual development. Iodine-thyronines perform their function by capturing iodine which is bound to particular amino acids in the adrenal gland. The ability to accumulate iodine is already present in some types of marine algae and is then developed by the first vertebrates. In reptiles it is this element that influences the shedding of the epidermis (transformation of state). In amphibians the thyroid determines the possibility of metamorphosis.

In mammals, the thyroid gland allows growth to be completed harmoniously. In man it allows to reach a normal intellectual level, to develop consciousness. Iodine is basically present in sea water, the primordial womb of life. In fact, iodine deficiency also leads to a lack of sexual maturation, i.e. a blockage of the activity of the second chakra. Furthermore, the adrenal cortex is also linked to memory and learning. The ability to capture calcium from the outside world and make it your own is, in fact, primitively linked to the kidney which is able to activate vitamin D, allowing it to bind calcium in the intestine. The fate of calcium, later, is instead directed by the thyroid gland. This gland, through the iodine-thyronines, therefore seems to guide and regulate, or rather to be the basis of a passage to a subsequent stage of psycho-physical development.

Via calcitonin, the thyroid has a hypocalcemic and hypophosphoremic effect: that is, it inhibits bone resorption and slows down the degradation of skeletal collagen, which leads to a decrease in hydroxyproline in the urine. Inhibits calcium loss. In other words, it promotes bone stability by directing calcium from the blood (hypocalcemia) towards the bone and retaining it in the kidneys. As for the parathyroids, their hormone is called parathyroid hormone (PTH). It has a complementary action to calcitonin, i.e. hypercalcemic.

Regulates the distribution of calcium and phosphorus in the bones (calcium hydroxyapatite). It promotes bone resorption activity, meaning that if there is a low level of calcium in the blood, PTH takes it from the bones and directs it into the blood. Furthermore, it favors its absorption from the external environment. PTH, in fact, mediates the synthesis of "activated" vitamin D. Every day 700-800 mg. of calcium can leave or enter the bones. Vitamin D, activated and transmitted to the intestine, allows the absorption of calcium and phosphates, whose subsequent fate is regulated by calcitonin and PTH.

In humans, with advancing age, there is a progressive reduction of calcium, intestinal absorption of calcium and calcitonin, and an increase in PTH which attempts to restore calcium. Does this lead to progressive osteoporosis, a rarefaction of matter, perhaps a preparation for a passage towards a more spiritual dimension? Examining the functions that distinguish these glands, we can say that the thyroid and parathyroids govern the "stability" of body matter, its greater or lesser "materialization" towards the synthesis of tissues, or energization towards the appearance and stabilization of the faculties intellectual and the creation of ideas, thus allowing man to express consciousness and self-awareness. In other words, they represent a nodal point of passage of energy from bottom to top and vice versa and of externalization of this transformed energy (for example, the formulation of ideas), just as we had seen happen by examining the functions expressed by the symbology of the corresponding chakra.

The anterior aspect of the fifth chakra is about expression and communication, but also the ability to take responsibility for one's actions and one's own. The malfunction of this fifth chakra can indicate the fear of receiving criticism from others or not being able to accept it without knowing how to face it or without being able to do it diplomatically. The conditions of this chakra inform us about the ability to let others know what we know, as well as our worth and our personality. The posterior aspect of the fifth chakra reflects our ability to receive, the image we have of ourselves, the security or insecurity in knowing how to carry out one's profession and also the satisfaction that one derives from it. Through this fifth chakra, thoughts, ideas and concepts from others are assimilated. If this chakra is weak, the person could let himself be influenced by the opinions of others without being able to adequately confront himself by comparing his own beliefs, but if it is too strong, the person will be able to open up with discernment to information arriving from the outside.

- If the color is in excess there will be anxious, introverted, shy, not inclined to form stable relationships, tending to escape from the situation, work relationships considered unrewarding.

If blue is at fault, you can be gossipy, critical, grumpy, unable to listen, irritable and touchy. Excess energy could cause: reduction in heart rate and increase in blood pressure, tiredness, melancholy. The blue energy defect could cause fever, acute pain mainly skeletal, menstrual pain, increased heart rate and decreased blood pressure, vein problems.

Indications:

- Agitation, distress, anxiety.
- Laryngitis - Laryngitis can be cured by drinking half a glass of blue solar water every half hour and gargling with the rest of the water, or by applying blue light directly to the throat.
- Inflammation - Blue rays have penetrating power and are excellent in the treatment of inflammatory disorders, in which case they exert a calming and refreshing action.
- Hypertension - Blue causes arteries, veins and capillaries to contract, thereby elevating blood pressure. The color acts in a particular way on the blood, producing a tonic effect. Blue is the color that generates balance and harmony; it is therefore able to bring the blood flow back to normal levels, when the blood is hyperactive and overheated.

- Tachycardia - Blue rays slow down cardiac activity and are therefore indicated in cases of tachycardia.
- Myopia - It is useful in the treatment of myopia both physically and psychologically, as it pushes the individual's ego outwards, expanding its field of orientation and bringing it into harmony with the environment.
- Aesthetics - In aesthetics it is mainly used in the case of thin, couperose skin.
- Pediatrics - In paediatrics, blue light (not ultraviolet) is the most powerful weapon to combat jaundice in newborns caused by accumulation of bilirubin. Before the completely accidental discovery of the action of the blue light beam, in cases of neonatal jaundice, total blood transfusion had to be carried out. Today, the blue light projected on the cradle, penetrating the epidermis, causes the breakdown of bilirubin in the blood vessels and thus the need for transfusion has been eliminated.

Contraindications:

- Depression - It has been verified that after ten minutes of treatment with blue rays, most subjects feel tired and depressed. Blue colored clothing and furnishings, if in a solid color and not broken by other colors, cause fatigue and depression in the body.

Blue is mainly used in offices and studios, as it promotes learning and thinking processes, and in bedrooms. Blue is a magical color that encourages and at the same time relaxes, soothes and inspires. Blue can, but need not, seem cold: the peace conveyed by the pale blue evokes the vastness of the summer sky and the image of an infinite space; the electrifying vitality of aquamarine and cobalt instead has a stimulating and refreshing effect; navy blue and denim are timeless classics. Some shades of blue look cooler than others, especially if you combine several shades of blue in one room. Warmer effects are obtained with natural tones such as Matisse blue, Savoy, turquoise, ultramarine or lilac.

Don't avoid blue just for fear it will make the environment too cold. There are blue tones that invite meditation, that give a sense of vastness and vitality or refinement. Be inspired by the beauty of flowers and leave room for the quiet of nature; take inspiration from the countries of the south, from the intense blue of the sky and the sea, from the lighter tones typical of the fishing villages in Greece and the Caribbean islands and from the dominant blue in the Mediterranean. These shades of blue exude a natural warmth and evoke the sun and the bright light of the south. A blue environment also represents learning ability and understanding. A study painted blue therefore stimulates learning and thinking. Blue is particularly suitable for decorating the bedroom, as it promotes deep and peaceful sleep. The blue-white combination is a classic that is always spot on.

Try to combine a few touches of orange, the complementary color of blue: next to yellow, red and terracotta; this combination immediately makes the shades of blue warmer. You can also easily combine steel blue with a cream colour, royal blue with emerald green, light blue with primrose yellow, denim with salmon or ultramarine with golden yellow.

Indigo

Indigo is a color that has always been considered very particular as it is the meeting point between blue and violet and is, contrary to the other colors of the spectrum, more of a shade than a real tint. Indigo is a powerful color and should be used sparingly. Its characteristics are similar to those of blue, but with a deeper effect, also due to its higher gradation and frequency. It is a symbol of spirituality, it represents the relationship with our inner abilities. Indigo influences our senses by improving mood in case of melancholy or light depressive states. Furthermore, the indigo color has a strong relaxing power and helps in meditative practices. This color acts positively on everything concerning the central nervous system and on all five senses. So it helps to significantly improve sight, hearing, touch, smell and taste. It acts on two glands that are important to us: the pituitary gland (pituitary gland, which regulates hormones and the metabolic activity of the whole body) and the pineal gland (epiphysis, which regulates the production of melatonin and the sleep-wake cycle). Anyone who loves indigo is a reserved, sensitive and imaginative person, internally rich, characterized by a dual inclination: on the one hand, he tends to isolate himself from the world, as a consequence of a critical judgment on the baseness of everyday reality, but on the other, in at the same time, he aspires to a communion of souls, out of a desire to find like-minded people. Indigo can be defined as the color of knowledge, balance, purification.

It is a color that enhances spirituality, but it is inadvisable, like all "cold" colors, for those who experience moments of fear or depression.

People who cannot harmonize with the world around them dislike the color indigo.

In Ayurvedic medicine it is used as an antidote to cobra venom.

Indigo is also a color with strong thermal insulating properties; it is no coincidence that the Tuaregs use tunics dyed with this color to better withstand the desert temperatures.

- Indigo is so relaxing that it is used as a pain reliever, be it physical or spiritual.
- It is good to use it in the meditation phase, when one is afflicted by problems and worries, when it seems to us that we have to face an insurmountable difficulty.
- Indigo is the color of solutions, because it helps to open the mind. It has a strong soothing power.

Indigo is a color of harmony that can be used at any time of the day, according to one's feelings. It is advisable to take a bath a day for at least 7 consecutive days, this to allow the body to recharge the energy of the colour, then reduce the use to 2/3 baths a week, according to one's needs.

Indigo is the color of the 6th chakra.

The sixth chakra is the brow chakra, third eye. It has two indigo lotus petals as its symbol and is placed in the center of the forehead, about two fingers above the root of the nose, in the position of the third eye. Its name in Sanskrit means to know, to perceive and also to command. It is the last chakra located within the physical body. On the two petals of the lotus are the letters Ham and Ksam. The sixth is the chakra of superior mental structure and superior vision, commonly called the third eye, considered fundamental in many oriental meditative practices (Tibet and India above all). It develops in adulthood. It expresses the right to see the truth, be it human or superior. It presides over the sense of sight.

In its anterior expression it is associated with the faculty of visualizing and making intellectual concepts comprehensible and, in its posterior expression, with the faculty of implementing the concepts themselves. If the sixth chakra is not harmonious, the person will easily find himself in a situation of confusion in which ideas and concepts will correspond to reality and consequently his actions, i.e. his ability to translate ideas into practice will fall or worse still, distorted ideas and concepts will be brought forward with the appropriate consequences for oneself and for others.

Perception, knowledge and command are the prerogatives of this chakra. It lets you enter the non-material world, the invisible, through extrasensory perception to bring knowledge and, therefore, deep awareness of what surrounds the human being, not only in matter and consequently allowing to command and guide your own existence. Speaking of this chakra, esoteric practice suggests that the spiritually highest Tibetan monks (lamas) undergo the surgical opening of the sixth chakra which allows them, not only to expand their consciousness, but also to connect with each other telepathically . They are also able to immediately and clearly recognize any negativity, as well as the spiritual potential, of the human beings they encounter. This center in the physical body is represented by the crossing of the two optic nerves in our brain (the "chiasm optic") and would control the functioning of the pituitary gland and the eyes. Excessive eyestrain (from cinema, television, computers or reading books) would harm this chakra which would also be damaged by bad thoughts.

This chakra would allow us to think about the future, create projects, develop extrasensory perceptions such as the ability to see without the use of the sense of sight, to reach mystical states, to perceive the so-called aura (a presumed field that would surround people, unknown to science, not to be confused with what is called aura in medicine) and to travel in the so-called "astral plane". The chakra would close in case of disappointments due to the failure to carry out a life project. The imbalances would manifest themselves through nightmares, uncontrolled or unpleasant psychic phenomena, complete lack of dreams, mental confusion and with diseases related to vision and frontal headaches.

The sixth Chakra represents thinking, it is also called the Third Eye Chakra. This is the seat of the highest mental faculties, intellectual abilities, as well as memory and will. By developing our awareness, and opening the third eye more and more, our imagination will be able to produce the energy necessary to realize our desires. When the Heart Chakra is open and in conjunction with the Third Eye Chakra, we can transmit our healing energies both from near and far. At the same time we can have access to all levels of creation, levels that go beyond even physical reality. Knowledge of this kind comes to us in the form of intuition, clairvoyance, and hypersensitivity to hearing and perceiving. Things that we had only vaguely suspected before now appear clearly to us.

This chakra rules dreams.

There are three types of dreams:

- Unconscious dreams, which bring up old issues from the subconscious so that we can gain a clearer understanding of how we really feel, rather than how we "should" feel. We may perceive these dreams as nightmares or as opportunities to be aware of our own darkness so it can be healed and released.
- Conscious dreams, which are often 'dress rehearsals' for what we are doing and trying to do in day life. After having these dreams we may feel tired, as if we have worked all night and, in a sense, we have.
- Superconscious dreams, which allow us to make real waking journeys through the inner planes. It is important to write down these dreams and integrate them into everyday life, as they are a true spiritual guide.

Even if a dream is not remembered, it still releases psychic tension. Research has shown that people who have received adequate sleep but have been deprived of dreams become disoriented and psychologically disturbed. It is even more beneficial if we learn to remember important dreams, because they give us important information about our SELF.

There are two effective ways to remember dreams. One: we say to ourselves, before falling asleep: "I will remember my dreams". Two: before we open our eyes in the morning, we tell ourselves what our dream was. This activity transfers dreams from the right cerebral hemisphere, the one that imagines, to the language areas of the left cerebral hemisphere. Then, often, we can remember the dreams long enough to write them down.

Some dreams are not difficult to remember and, in fact, haunt us until we process them to a full understanding of their meaning.

The consciousness of this chakra opens and drops the "veil of maya", the illusion of worldly appearances. It would also represent the power to see-know what hasn't happened yet, but is about to happen. In the sector identified by this chakra are the diencephalon and two glands of fundamental importance for the control and regulation of the whole organism, the pituitary and the epiphysis, i.e. the pituitary and pineal glands. Both manifest within our body as our ego and superego. The pituitary gland hangs about in the center of the lower part of the brain, below the third ventricle, and is housed in a niche of the sphenoid bone called, due to its shape, the sella turcica. It is composed of two fundamental parts, of ectodermal derivation: the neuro-hypophysis, derived from the floor of the diencephalon (it contains a recess of the third ventricle), and the adeno-hypolysis, derived from the vault of the stomodeum, i.e. from the primitive buccal cavity.

In some animal species, as evidence of this derivation and of the primitive site of elimination of the pituitary secretion, a communication duct remains between the pituitary and the buccal cavity (in some fish; in some reptiles and birds only a closed cord remains). These ancestral ways of communication between compartments of the body, which appear completely separate in humans, force us to reflect on the words of yogis who claim they can reactivate normally closed paths and communications within the body. The hormones of the pituitary gland are STH-growth hormone; TSH-thyroid stimulating hormone; ACTH-hormone that stimulates the adrenocortical; FSH-hormone that stimulates the growth of the ovarian follicle; LH-hormone that stimulates the corpus luteum (interstitial cells in males); PRL-hormone that stimulates lactation. The hormone of the middle part is the melanocyte-stimulating hormone MSH (regulates skin pigmentation). The neuro-hypophysis does not synthesize hormones, but accumulates and releases the neuro-secretions accumulated by the hypothalamus; the most important are oxytocin, which stimulates uterine contractions and the release of milk from the udder, and vasopressin, which stimulates water reabsorption in the kidney.

As you can see, the pituitary controls the whole body, because it controls the endocrine glands. What happens in the diencephalon-pituitary system therefore prefigures the bodily or psychic modifications that will manifest themselves in the individual. A dysfunction of this system will therefore lead to an imbalance in all the psycho-physical functions of the individual. Observing the role of the pituitary gland in the body we can say, using a figurative language but relevant to reality, that this gland (or rather, the diencephalon-pituitary system) represents "the established order", the "royalty" that governs, the ability to prefigure, project, integrate, control all the functions of the body, or, for yoga, what exists in the «microcosm».

The epiphysis is a small pine cone-shaped gland less than 1 cm long and weighing 150 g, located at the level of the posterior wall of the third ventricle, to which it is connected via a peduncle, such as the pituitary. Going up the evolutionary ladder, above the amphibians the pineal becomes essentially glandular, although still little known sensory cells remain, and the main hormone it produces is melatonin which is rhythmically secreted following the light-dark cycles of the external environment, even if the gland is no longer in direct contact with the external source of light (for example, in humans). It is as if his visual function, previously direct, had been able to internalize itself. In fact, the pineal receives an afferent innervation from the superior cervical ganglion of the sympathetic, which in turn is connected to the eye. The perception of darkness causes melatonin synthesis which, by inducing the aggregation of melanin granules in the skin, lightens the skin.

Light, on the other hand, decreases sympathetic nerve impulses and blocks hormone synthesis: a few minutes of exposure to bright light are enough to cause a drop in circulating levels of melatonin. The integrity of this pathway is essential for the activity of the gland. Following the light-dark rhythms, the epiphysis in fact synchronizes and synchronizes the whole organism on the rhythms of day and night, of the seasons, etc., that is, on the rhythms of the macrocosm that surrounds it.

The epiphysis would therefore be an internal-external "synchronizer", a guide of the temporal structure of the organism: regardless of the vision, the organism knows if it is day or night or in which period of the year we are. At the same time, the epiphysis dictates the rhythm of the internal "seasons":

melatonin decreases in puberty, during ovulation, in menopause, in old age.

All this through a transformation of the light impulse which, materializing, becomes a hormonal impulse. Light, nerve impulse, epiphysis, hormone: the coagulating function of Saturn of the alchemists, the third eye of the Orient. At the current state of research, epiphyseal biorhythms seem to control mood, hormonal balance, immune balance and appear to have an anti-stress action. In summary, the organic functions corresponding to this chakra are control over the balance of the entire psycho-soma, control of the ability to self-recognize or maintain the integrity of one's individuality, the internalization of visual abilities previously directed towards the outside , with greater possibility of self-adjustment and self-synchronization. As always, we find a correspondence between the symbolism of the chakra and the functions of the organs included in its wheel. If the functions are these, it is even more understandable how the opening of this chakra allows one to have consciousness and control over the entire human microcosm, to lift the veil of maya, the illusions, freeing the individual from the "spectre of the dragon uroboric», that is, total unconsciousness, which always tries to reabsorb it into itself.

- If indigo is in excess there will be moments of distraction, you may be led to daydreaming, barred in action, with fantastical fixations and beliefs. The excess of indigo energy could therefore cause episodes of hallucination, illusions, obsessions, nightmares.

- If the indigo is at fault you will be insensitive, with poor memory and poor imagination, visualization difficulties, inability to remember dreams, tendency to deny the evidence. The lack of indigo energy would cause vision problems, skin alterations often on an emotional basis, tears easily.

Indications:
- It is a purifier of the circulatory system, including blood, and also a mental purifier.

- It is useful for eye inflammation, ear and hearing diseases.
- By projecting an indigo-colored ray into the ear of those suffering from tinnitus (ringing or ringing in the ears), the disease can be eradicated.
- In fevers associated with dysfunctions of the lymphatic system, it is radiated to the groin and under the armpits.
- Many sportsmen adopt it to tone up the muscle, as indigo purifies the blood and improves the tissues, even on the surface.
- Promotes the production of phagocytes in the spleen.

Contraindications:
- Subjects who tend to take charge of everyone's problems.
- Introspective people who often suffer from anxiety attacks or nightmares.
- Depression.

Purple

Located near the ultraviolet gradations, purple (complementary of yellow) is the color with the highest frequency and the greatest penetration and for this reason it has always been considered the color of the spirit, stimulating subtle energies, the unconscious, creativity and of intuition. Known since ancient times as the color of the spirit, it is associated with magic, stillness and silence which open up to intuition.

- It is the color that brings together masculine and feminine energy.

Leonardo da Vinci claimed that his capacity for meditation and contemplation increased when he was in a church with purple glass in the windows. In fact, purple stimulates meditation and acts on the psyche and the unconscious dimension, giving spiritual strength and inspiration. In the light spectrum, the color Purple is positioned at the antipodes of Red and symbolizes the ability to identify with others. It is the ray with the greatest energetic properties of the visible spectrum. Born from the mix of red (love) and blue (wisdom) it is the color of metamorphosis, transition, mystery and magic. Purple is made up of blue and red and as such helps balance both ends of the spectrum. Furthermore, since warm colors are associated with masculine energy and cold ones with feminine energy, purple can be used to harmonize these two energies, these two sides of the character present in each of us. It is the color of spirituality but also of erotic fascination, it indicates the union of opposites, suggestibility. Purple often represents wealth and justice and passivity. In the spectrum, purple ranks behind blue. Like green, purple is a color that contains yin and yang, the heat of red and the cold of blue.

- It is excellent for deep meditation, therefore to free the mind from all activity and to obtain a better inner vision of oneself.
- Purple is the color of Neptune and Pisces, and one of the colors of Jupiter and Sagittarius.

In nature, its various shades are mixtures of red and blue; therefore also in occult symbolism, it is to be considered in this color, the presence of red, color of Fire and of life, and that of blue, air, Heaven. Today, as in antiquity, purple represents the transition between life and immortality. It is spirituality veiled by a tinge of sadness or melancholy, which implies the remembrance of earthly things.

- Those who love the color Purple are pervaded by a strong desire to be accepted and to please the people around them. He usually denotes a disposition to be apprehensive and awkward but also wishes to be understood and to be treated kindly. Those who prefer Viola find it difficult to control their emotional level but they also know how to set aside too much rationality. Lover of art in all its forms, he adores the strong sensations that come from contact with the environment and people.
- Those who shun the color Purple tend to be distrustful and overly critical of everyone. He makes rationality and logic his weapon capable of protecting him from any type of emotional state.
- If this color is found in excess, one will be fragile, emotional, confused, hyper-rational, mystical, visionary. The excess of violet energy could cause alterations in the state of consciousness, emotional disturbances, drowsiness.
- The purple color in default will make materialists, skeptics, greedy, apathetic, dominators. The purple energy defect could cause water retention, venous and lymphatic circulation disorders.

Purple is the color of the 7th chakra.

The seventh chakra is the crown chakra, the vertex center.
Its color is purple, gold, white.
Its symbol is the lotus with a thousand petals, where one thousand is the result of 50 x 20: the fifty phonemes of the

Sanskrit alphabet repeated twenty times, and it is located at the top of the skull, in the Bregma area.

It is a non-physical Chakra, which can essentially be defined as the interface between the individual consciousness and the cosmic, universal one. It is here, in this chakra, that the adept experiences union with the divine, liberation, samadhi.

It is a non-physical Chakra, which can essentially be defined as the interface between the individual consciousness and the cosmic, universal one. There is no blocked seventh Chakra, it can only be more or less developed, in relation to the individual's personal spiritual path. There are no known and specific pathologies related to this energy center, neither on a physical nor on a mental or spiritual level; we only know that the energy elaborated at this level has effects on all the tissues and functions of the organism, in a more or less evident, intense and effective way. The crown chakra controls the cerebrum, crown of the head, the entire brain and nervous system. It is also said to control the right eye. In Egyptian mythology, the opened Third Eye is called the Eye of Horus.

- The physical left eye controls the Moon and the manifested and feminine worlds and the right eye controls the unmanifested, masculine and spiritual worlds.

Thus, the Right Eye of Horus descends Spirit into matter and then feeds that Spirit into the Left Eye of Horus. In this way, the Third Eye remains open, grounded in the physical world and fully receptive. It is the chakra that connects with one's most spiritual part, and with cosmic reality.

- Reaching the opening and awareness of this chakra leads to the completeness of being only if it is reached through the opening and awareness of all the other chakras, without exception.

- On the other hand, the disharmony of the seventh chakra leads to a closure and a non-understanding of the spiritual part, both one's own and that of others with, as a consequence, a decidedly materialistic vision of existence.

The seventh chakra is the Light of knowledge and awareness, it is a global vision of the Universe and in everyone's growth path it can lead to the spiritual serenity of complete, universal knowledge. The seventh chakra is what brings the human being closest to total contact with his own interiority and, therefore, with the divine. It's the chakra that pushes the most aware people to try to elevate their self and connect with the Whole. Meeting a human being with the seventh chakra completely open means meeting someone absolutely out of the ordinary: a true Master.

- Only Jesus, Buddha, Osho, Mahavira, Krishna are recognized as Masters who have reached enlightenment, a level of spirituality so high that they do not need to speak.

It is enough to look at them to follow them unconditionally. It would be located in the pineal gland and made up of the meeting of the six chakras. It would be a hollow space, on the edges of which there would be a thousand nerves. These nerves could be seen by sectioning the brain cross-sectionally. Prior to self-realization, this center is closed by the ego and superego. Illuminated by the awakening of the kundalini, it would become similar to a bundle of flames of seven colors which integrate eventually creating a clear crystal color flame. This would correspond to absolute freedom, joy of spirit, serenity, the relationship between the consciousness of the individual and that of the universe. This chakra would close in the event of a "near fainting" to prevent loss of consciousness and the soul from escaping. Physically it would manifest itself with vitiligo and vertigo and in the psychological field with boredom, dissatisfaction, hatred towards God. It has in its heart a smaller lotus with twelve petals in which the triangle called Kamakala is inscribed, which symbolically represents the seat of the Supreme Shakti, i.e. the unindividualized "cosmic force". It is located above the end of Sushumna; some master specifies in the middle of the brain, some others say just below the brahmarandhra, while others place it just above this. Sahasrara appears as a white lotus with luminous filaments, with "a thousand petals".

Inside the full moon shines among cold silvery rays and inside it is inscribed the triangle that houses the great void, origin and dissolution of everything. Here resides Paramashiva, symbol of the identification between the individual soul and the universal soul, between man and God, realization of the supreme bliss that follows the destruction of ignorance and false vision operated by Paramashiva himself as the supreme guru who instructs the devoted yogi. The crown chakra governs not only the brain's control of our entire nervous system, but also our Higher Self's control of our entire physical incarnation. Once the crown chakra is open, we can become aware of our true "brain" that exists beyond the limitations of the third and fourth dimensions. Our ability to perceive physical life from that higher perspective allows us to gain access to our multidimensional consciousness. While in that multidimensional state, we have the ability to see the myriad forms of our existence in the many different planes and realities. The crown chakra rules Cosmic Consciousness which is our connection to spiritual wisdom, aspirations and knowledge of Truth. From this perspective, we see ourselves as a spark of consciousness that creates all and, paradoxically, "IS" all. From our Cosmic Consciousness, we are the dreamer dreaming a dream and realizing that all that is perceived is an extension of our Self. Just as the root chakra represents our connection to the Divine Mother or Mother Earth, the crown chakra represents our relationships to the Divine Father or Sky Father. Father Sky and Mother Earth unite, Spirit in Matter, to create the Child of Love, consciousness in physical form. Mother Earth in the first chakra roots our power and sends it upwards from the earth to unite with Father Sky in the seventh chakra. The rising of the Kundalini connects us with the energy that comes from the higher dimensions while giving us the power and responsibility, in turn, to ground that energy into the physical plane. The relationship with the mother is associated with the first chakra. If the connection with our mother was not sufficient for our needs, we often feel cut off from our roots, from physical life and our attitudes towards home, security and money are negatively affected. Conversely, the relationship with the human father is associated with the seventh chakra. Since the crown chakra represents our unity with life, we feel a sense of isolation from "God" and humanity if the bond with our father is insufficient. Because the crown chakra represents our multidimensional consciousness, when we open it our reality is no longer limited to the third and fourth dimensions. When the third eye chakra, the sixth chakra opens, we begin to travel to the higher sub-planes of the fourth dimension. With the opening of the seventh chakra, and subsequent activation of the Third Eye, consciousness can now enter the fifth dimension. It is then that the many realities around and within us gradually become apparent to us. Opening the crown chakra expands our perception into the fifth dimension where there is no polarity. Thus, there are many paradoxes associated with this chakra, as it represents the "end of all paradox". As we journey through the higher dimensions, it is important to release all judgments associated with the polarities of light and dark. Instead, we must consult our inner awareness and higher consciousness to navigate us through our inner worlds. Eventually, we will all be aware of our fifth dimensional selves, they know no judgment and have no fear. He makes rationality and logic his weapon capable of protecting him from any type of emotional state. The wearer denotes dignity and nobility, intelligence, prudence, humility and wisdom. The character is a bit difficult with opposite and irreconcilable tendencies. He needs to feel free, he wants to fascinate, he arouses sympathy and admiration everywhere. He is very available and communicative, has great humanity, cultivates high-level, cultured and sensitive interests. He desires to help others in a meaningful way, has an inclination for the occult, the magical and the arcane. He has good taste and takes great care of his physical appearance. Refined lover of beauty and art.

Indications:
- Violet facilitates the balance between sodium and potassium, contributing to bone development.
- Stimulates lymphatic circulation and proper functioning of the spleen, kidneys and bladder.
- Stimulates the production of white blood cells, the spleen, the osteo-skeletal development.

- Blood purification, it slows down cardiac activity and promotes cerebral microcirculation, for this reason it is used to counteract baldness.
- In aesthetics it is mainly used in the case of skin with freckles, with oxidation spots, presence of widespread oiliness. It is active in dermatosis in general. Excellent healer.

Contraindications:
- Mental disorders - Increases loss of sense of reality.
- Depression, insanity.

Those who wear purple essentially convey fantasy and spirituality. If purple is very dark it can mean interest in esotericism. This color is also suitable for those who want to be original, without being loud. Being a mix of blue and red (on opposite sides) it is an indication of the desire to stand out from the crowd. In clothing, the lighter shades express sensuality, the darker spirituality, because purple derives from the fusion of blue, sacred, and red, profane.

White

White is the combination of all colors of the electromagnetic spectrum. By passing the color white through a crystal prism, a rainbow of colors is created. Together they form the color white. The color white is a color without tint, but which has a high luminosity. It is the symbol of purity, virginity, spirituality and divinity. White is also the color of angels, eternity and heaven. In the celebration of the marriage the brides are dressed in white just like the white dress of the person being baptized. White is a color that revitalizes: fresh, bright, sunny, if worn it brings energy and vigor. White is the symbol of purity, innocence and naivety. A person who wears white constantly has a personality that tends towards perfectionism and idealism. Often, in fact, he chases after unrealizable ideas and dreams. Conversely, if white is worn with other colors, it indicates a vital and balanced personality. White is the completeness of colors, without having color. White is also the color of wisdom and old age; in fact, the hoary elderly people represent the wisdom due to the long experience of life lived.

- Those who love white reveal a marked tendency towards fatalism, but at the same time express creativity and imagination. Those who prefer white have a continuous desire for change and are stimulated by the novelties that life presents them. He has great faith in others and in everything that the future holds for him but, at the same time, he can create illusions and sin of naivety.

- Those who reject white do not trust others very much and believe that the future should be written without leaving the reins of the games to chance or "fate". Often stuck in his positions, he doesn't like news and is reluctant to make abrupt changes in his life. Very pragmatic and rational, those who cannot stand white hardly leave room for imagination and sensitivity of mind.

It is the opposite of black, with which you chase like keys on a piano or boxes on a chessboard. It is the color of brides, of milk, but also of ghosts and nights spent without sleep. In fact, if in the Western tradition white is the color of peace, in the Eastern tradition it is the color of mourning and ghosts, as for example in Chinese civilization. The word white is used in the common sense to indicate Western peoples, the white flag is the symbol of surrender, of armistice. White is the color of snow and hair in old age. It is the right color to mark a new beginning, a transition.

- Combined with silver, it symbolizes the moon and femininity.
- Associated with black it is a symbol of duality
- Associated with red it symbolizes the devil and purgatory.

In the psychology of the traditions of some peoples, white also represents negative values. In Victorian England, to receive a white feather is to be considered a coward. The first aid, the white color means no urgency and therefore the green code and above all the red code take precedence.

Black

Black is the color worn by those who want to appear interesting and cultured. Black is the color of the mysterious and inexplicable. Black is light that has not yet manifested itself, in black everything exists but is not visible, therefore black symbolizes all that is hidden. If a person dresses almost exclusively in black or surrounds himself excessively in this color it means that he is stifling his own intimate desires. Those who love black are irrational, rebellious, authoritarian, hasty. He loves elegance.

- Those who prefer the color black argue that the future holds few favorable opportunities for them and are convinced that the responsibility for everything rests with the world in which they live and with society. From these hidden beliefs it follows an apparently defeatist behavior that can lead to angry rebellions.

- Those who repudiate black want to express the desire for freedom and not to be commanded by others, not to be dominated and not to give up anything. Usually those who reject the black sin of altruism and, indeed, often expects from others much more than what he can do for others.

In Ancient Egypt the color black was considered one of the colors sacred to the deity. The greatest Masters used it as a symbol of primordial Unity, where everything was essence, potential strength and equality. The black color represents total realization and the Absolute. As a symbol of spiritual authority, this reflects part of divinity, conveys sobriety, concentration, austerity and dignity. It is the symbol of full knowledge and integration of consciousness with the universe. The color black is a sacred color because it represents eternal rest, the pacified soul that is immersed in the fullness of being. It represents the occultum, that is, what is hidden and must be "discovered" and brought to light, or hidden in the sense of being protected.

- The black color in chromotherapy is connected to the feet chakra. It therefore channels the primordial energies, which make the existence of matter possible. Black in this case only takes on the meaning of pure chaos/energy that can be modelled, melted and subsequently radiated.

For the ancient Egyptians, for example, the color black was considered sacred to the deities and the Masters used to use it as a symbol of Unity, pure Essence and equality. It was seen as the total achievement, the symbol of the highest authority. Symbol of knowledge and interaction with the Universe. Black therefore, in chromotherapy, has a very positive meaning. It is the connection with the Divine Mother and with the earth. Something that is not to be feared, but rather explored. The black stones in crystallotherapy reconfirm the "good reputation" of this color. The ancient matriarchal cults valued these minerals because they contained the mystery of the universe and the energies that govern it. According to a marvelous legend, it is from the explosion of a tiny black onyx that all creation came to life. Each mere crystal therefore, could potentially contain entire universes. Another legend has it that, always in the onyx, the divinities sleep asleep. In short, black stones work like a sponge. They absorb negative energies, filter them and release protection and positivity. They help remove energy blockages. These energies are then radiated upon the physical plane.

Brown

Obtained from the combination of Red, Yellow and Black, the Brown color is a symbol of physical satisfaction. This color is the result of the vitality of the red color purified by the awareness of Yellow and, Yellow and Red together, attenuate the sense of rebellion expressed by the color Black. Brown therefore, the result of this combination, expresses emotion and sensuality, but also, balance, good health and need for sensual satisfaction. Brown is therefore the color of strong, solid people with great stamina and patience. In general, these are very conscientious people, that is, aware of their duty and responsibility, they are constant, attentive and conservative. The brown-type is perhaps a little slow to understand and to act but in the end he gets what he wants.

- Those who choose the Brown color have a constant need to feel good about their body and are constantly looking for harmony. Generally, those who prefer Brown are positive and satisfied with the life they lead. Those who love brown are trustworthy, calm, thoughtful and dislike change. He doesn't like news and tries to have a stable relationship with his partner; the problem with these people is their low mobility and inability to adapt quickly. It is a warm color and represents the color of Mother Earth, of wood, for which it is associated with solid and lasting things. The preference for brown symbolizes the lack of roots but at the same time helps to be practical and non-dispersive. It is excellent as a color in floors because it represents the earth, from stability.

- Those who refuse Brown do not put the satisfactions deriving from physical well-being in the foreground while they always tend to excel by not allowing themselves any kind of weakness. He loves that his deeds are approved by the people he cares about most and is constantly worried about disappointing the expectations that others place in him as a person.

If you dream of the brown color it means that you feel insecure and therefore you are looking for a safe, calm and full of human warmth environment. People who have brown eyes are intelligent, funny and very sweet.
They often lack individuality and absolutely do not want to attract attention. This color indicates a person who likes corporality and who is very much directed towards physical pleasures.

Gray

It is a color that is neither dark nor light, it is devoid of any stimulus. It is the color of closure and non-involvement, of prudence and compromise. Anyone who loves gray is intelligent, thoughtful, introverted, unfriendly, shy and therefore hardly gets involved. People who frequently wear this color tend to judge and condemn others.

- Those who prefer Gray are not serene and try, in every situation that presents themselves, to take time or in any case to detach themselves from contexts that can cause them anxiety and emotional tension. Furthermore, those who appreciate the color Gray have a character that does not adapt to the circumstances with the risk of being set aside, thus increasing that feeling of inadequacy which leads them to behave in a disinterested way towards everything they do.

- Anyone who shuns the color Gray is usually a very busy individual in various activities both for personal gain and for fear of being ousted. Those who reject the Gray are in a perpetual state of tension and are afraid of anything that is not tangible or unknown.

The gray color is obtained by combining black and white. Depending on the different concentrations of the two colors, different shades of gray are obtained. This color is also obtained by mixing blue, yellow and red in equal quantities. Another way to obtain gray is to mix cyan, magenta and yellow in equal parts, which are the three main printing colors. Gray is a neutral color.
It is the color of the fog, of the ash, of the hair of people of a certain age. It is the color of monotony and sadness. In tailoring, even if it's a neutral color, it can become elegant and sexy, using appropriate combinations.

It goes well with soft colors, high visibility colors, but it is better to avoid combinations with white, brown and beige.

Gray is used to produce lenses because by uniformly absorbing the spectrum of visible light, it allows to maintain excellent visibility. The same goes for windshield manufacturers who use it in the upper part, obtaining a good reduction of solar glare.

Pink

An ambivalent symbol of heavenly perfection and earthly passion. The color pink comes from the mingling of the power of red and the neutrality of white and has always universally represented sweetness and delicacy, but also gratitude, understanding and tenderness. In fact, it is also the symbol of newborns, regardless of gender and is used to paint the walls of the rooms where the little ones sleep.

Contrary to what one might think today, for centuries pink has been considered a color suitable for males because in most cultures, not just oriental ones, it was a variant of red, a symbol of male strength and virility which was combined with white, representing spirituality and purity of soul. Only in more recent years has it instead been associated with the female sex, while blue has become the color of males since birth, even if in reality specific medical research has shown that children up to at least three years of age do not distinguish pink from red .

- Those who prefer pink are capable of great passionate loves where they give all of themselves with total self-sacrifice. He has a strong desire to understand his partner and love him with all of himself until he vanishes. Those who love the color pink prefer muffled and ethereal environments and want to be in the company of people who express tenderness. The greatest dowry for those who prefer this color is the ease with which they can come into contact with everything around them through the senses. Anyone who loves pink is a calm, optimistic, thoughtful person who doesn't hold a grudge against others.

- Those who reject pink are afraid to come out and show their weak side for fear of being hurt. This fear can lead the individual to withdraw into himself without showing the tender and loving side of him. The consequence of this attitude can lead the person to be dry and hard.

Furthermore, those who shun pink are wary of sensual nuances and prefer the clarity of reason.

The pink color is linked to the meanings of beauty, grace, happiness, fertility, love, but without sensuality. It symbolizes passionless love and affection. The person who prefers pink wants protection, delicacy and affection. The color pink like the rose plant is associated with the heart-center. It is considered the other color of Venus. In psychology pink is the symbol of hope. It is therefore a positive color that instills a certain sense of security and optimism towards the future. A color that calms primitive instincts, mitigates feelings of anger and aggression, but also the sense of abandonment and the desire for revenge towards others. Contrary to red, which universally and not only in medicine is considered the color of energy, of sudden action, pink instead conveys tranquility and the desire to think before acting.

Everyday sensations and impressions are associated with the color pink. Its main feature is to relax the mind, but also to demonstrate open-mindedness towards others, the desire to collaborate with others.

Colors and clothing

The use of colors is also very important in clothing.
The amount of energy of each color is inversely proportional to the wavelength. The higher the wavelength, the stronger the skin penetration and the lower the energy charge. Thus, red is the most penetrating color, then there will be orange, yellow, green, blue, indigo and violet. The latter reaches limited depths, but infuses a high amount of energy.

- Red - Temperament sometimes aggressive. Those who wear red are undoubtedly noticed. Red can also be linked to aggression or sexual incontinence. Indicated for circulatory problems (stasis, chilblains, coldness). Very useful is the use of socks and red gloves to improve peripheral circulation. In male impotence it is very useful to wear red briefs or swimsuits.
- Orange-The wearer expresses joy and self-affirmation, good humor and altruism. Recommended for rheumatics and as an activator of the intestine (constipation). For women who have difficulty conceiving due to psychological problems. Remember that the electromagnetic energy of orange is on the same vibrational frequency as the DNA chain.
- Yellow - Those who wear yellow feel good about themselves; it is, in fact, the color associated with the sense of identity, with the ego, with extroversion. always denotes a strong personality. Using it stimulates rationality and the left brain, improves gastric functions and tones the lymphatic system.
- Green - It is the color of energy balance. The wearer seeks balance and reflection. Its effect is relaxing and refreshing, so in case of migraine or insomnia.
- Light blue - People who wear light blue tend towards introversion and a certain external closure. It is the color of the phlegmatic temperament.

- Indigo - Suitable for particularly tense and nervous people. It is worn by reserved and very closed people who want to live in their world.
- Purple - The lighter shades express sensuality, the darker spirituality. It includes blue and red (sacred and profane). It is strongly contraindicated in depression.
- Black - Slims the figure. It can be worn in the evening but avoided during the day, as it blocks the penetration of the electromagnetic radiation of the colors into the skin and exchanges with the outside world. It is a color that tends to devitalize the person and in the case of underwear to cool sexuality and in the long run to damage the reproductive sphere. It enhances red (strength and power), with yellow it enhances intellectual power and with pink social power. Black is to be avoided in case of depression.
- White - Revitalizes the whole organism. It is a fresh and sunny color that brings energy.
- Gray - People who wear gray put a barrier between themselves and the world. It was the color of the authorities who wanted to put a clear detachment from the "rest".
- Brown - The preference for brown symbolizes lack of roots but at the same time helps to be practical and non-dispersive.

The Chromoesthetics

Chromoesthetics consists in irradiating areas of the body with light of different colors to obtain an aesthetic advantage. It can be integrated with traditional beauty treatments in order to enhance and speed up the final result. It is a new methodology that considers blemishes as a disharmonious vibration of the cells of a certain area of the body which can be rebalanced by exploiting the energy and, therefore, the vibration of one or more specific colours.

In Chromoesthetics, before acting, it is necessary to identify the imperfection by evaluating its characteristics in order to choose the right color or colors to proceed with its repair. With the energy of color it is therefore possible to exert a global influence on the body in particular through the skin and once the physical dysfunction has been eliminated, the way of thinking and emotion in general are changed. Thanks to its completeness and specificity, Cromoesthetics is ideal for treating the health and beauty of the body and mind

Chromoesthetics can be applied according to 3 methods:

1. The first consists of a natural treatment of the blemish by projecting the color directly onto the skin making the two vibrations interact with each other (blemish/colour). In fact, the light energy with its frequency reacts with the disharmonious vibrations of the blemish bringing the skin back to its right cellular balance.

    In fact, the altered function of a cell body (e.g. facial skin) is found in an intercellular oscillatory change with the consequent dysfunctions due to a complex chemical-physical interaction variation between cell and cell (e.g. decrease in collagen production). By interacting with the right frequency of colored light, cellular homeostasis can be restored with the result of remission of the chemical-physical variation and the consequent better biological function.

2. The second consists in strengthening the classic aesthetic treatments, i.e. those that involve dexterity combined with the use of the product.

This is mainly based on the irradiation, with the appropriate color, of the product already applied. It is effective, and therefore produces clearly visible results, since, based on the interaction between the energy of the colour, the skin and the product, it determines that:

- The action of the active ingredient of the product is enhanced.
- The product is conveyed more easily and quickly.
- The skin becomes more receptive and therefore absorbs the product better.
- Smaller quantities of product are used. Cosmetic products related to Cromoesthetics must have specific characteristics that are not found in all products.

3. The third methodology consists in the interaction of the two previous methodologies. In this case, the skin must be irradiated with the appropriate color(s) in order to prepare it for treatment with cosmetic products. In this case there is already a beneficial effect on the imperfection which will be further enhanced with the application of the specific product and with its subsequent irradiation using the suitable colour. According to tests and researches, this methodology is the most effective and the one that can also produce the best effect (relaxation or revitalization depending on the colour) on the person.

The qualities of the single colors of the iris in aesthetic applications:

- Red

It is called the great energetic.

It is active in edema, temporary swelling, lymphatic and blood stasis. In the aesthetic field it is mainly used in cases of rough, intoxicated, edematous skin as well as in nodular cellulite (if not accompanied by circulatory imbalance).

- Orange

It symbolizes the rising sun.
In aesthetics it is mainly used in the case of oily, young skin with an intermediate acneic tendency, comedonic skin, thick skin. It is active in opaque and discolored epidermis; in imperfections (hypothenia, cellulite, adiposity) due to an imbalance in the digestive processes and altered functionality of the endocrine system. It works in cases of soft oedematous cellulite. Promotes hair shine; acts on greasy dandruff from sebaceous hypersecretion.

- Yellow

It is the color of rationality. In aesthetics it is mainly used in case of oily, asphyxiated, mature acneic skin and in lymphatic stasis. It is often active combined with other colors in impure skin with an acneic tendency, in asphyxiated, stressed and toneless epidermis. Activate the lymphatic system; purifies the liver, intestines and skin and purifies the blood.

- Green

It is the color of serenity. In aesthetics it is mainly used in case of dry, alipic, relaxed withered, wrinkled, elderly, senescent, fragile, dehydrated skin. It is the building block of muscles and tissues. It is active in premature aging of the skin, wrinkles, sagging skin, undernutrition, dehydration, dyschromia. It works in cases of connective tissue weakness.

- Blue

It is the color of relaxation. In aesthetics, it is mainly used in the case of couperose skin, thin, with dilated pores, contracted, congested. It has antiseptic and bactericidal properties; it is soothing in burns and redness from heat. It acts on stress wrinkles and contracted features. It is also active in stress cellulite.

- Indigo

It is the color of sublimation. In aesthetics it is mainly used in the case of toneless, inelastic, pimply, sensitive, fissured skin. It is soothing in irritation due to prolonged sun exposure. Restores the natural tone to the fabrics. It is refreshing, astringent, haemostatic.

- Violet

It is the color of meditation. In aesthetics it is mainly used in the case of skin with freckles, with oxidation spots, presence of widespread oiliness. It is active in dermatosis in general.

Aesthetic chrome treatments for the face:
- Acne-prone skin
- Asphyxiated skin
- Atonic skin
- Couperose skin
- Dehydrated skin
- Oily skins
- Mature skin
- Peeling with lifting effect
- Wrinkles
- Facial skin renewal.

Aesthetic chrome treatments for the body:
- Skin renewal
- Hands
- Breast relaxed
- Nodular cellulitis
- Edemic and soft cellulite
- Localized weight loss.

Polychromatic Optical Group (POG)

This innovative lighting system allows you to illuminate and color environments, people and objects in a uniform way and without shadows. POG technology is capable of producing shades of natural light that can be broken down into the colors of the rainbow which help regenerate tissues and reactivate them on an energy level. It is a light that envelops the person in an embrace of colour, it does not dazzle even if looked at directly and continuously.

The use of colors is also very important in furnishing.
- Living room: orange
- Study: yellow
- Bedroom: pink, blue or green
- Kitchen: turquoise or yellow
- Bathroom: turquoise
- Offices: light yellow
- Ballrooms: red or orange
- Schools: yellow or green.

The use of colors is also very important in clothing.

- Red

Temperament sometimes aggressive. Those who wear red are undoubtedly noticed. Red can also be linked to aggression or sexual incontinence. Indicated for circulatory problems (stasis, chilblains, coldness). Very useful is the use of socks and red gloves to improve peripheral circulation.
In male impotence it is very useful to wear red briefs or swimsuits.

- Orange

The wearer expresses joy and self-affirmation, good humor and altruism. For women who have difficulty conceiving due to psychological problems. Remember that the electromagnetic energy of orange is on the same vibrational frequency as the DNA chain.

- Yellow

Those who wear yellow feel good about themselves; it is in fact the color associated with the sense of identity, with the ego, with extroversion. Always denotes a strong personality. Using it stimulates rationality and the left brain, improves gastric functions and tones the lymphatic system.

- Green

It is the color of energy balance. The wearer seeks balance and reflection. Its effect is relaxing and refreshing, so in case of migraine or insomnia.

- Light blue

People who wear light blue tend towards introversion and a certain external closure. It is the color of the phlegmatic temperament.

- Dark Blue (Indigo)

Suitable for particularly tense and nervous people. It is worn by reserved and very closed people who want to live in their world.

- Purple

The lighter shades express sensuality, the darker spirituality. It includes blue and red (sacred and profane). It is strongly contraindicated in depression.

- Black

Slims the figure. It can be worn in the evening but avoided during the day, as it blocks the penetration of the electromagnetic radiation of the colors into the skin and exchanges with the outside world. It is a color that tends to devitalize the person and in the case of underwear to cool sexuality and in the long run to damage the reproductive sphere. Black is to be avoided in case of depression.

- White

Revitalizes the whole organism.
It is a fresh and sunny color that brings energy.

- Grey

People who wear gray put a barrier between themselves and the world. It was the color of the authorities who wanted to put a clear detachment from the "rest".

- Brown

The preference for brown symbolizes lack of roots but at the same time helps to be practical and non-dispersive.

The Chromopuncture

Chromopuncture was born from the combination of the theories of chromotherapy with those of acupuncture; branch of chromotherapy, little known and certainly less practiced than acupuncture, it carries out its action by working on the same somatic points exploited by Chinese medicine. What is different is the method of soliciting the points which, if in the case of acupuncture it occurs through the use of needles, in chromopuncture it takes place through the action of the characteristic wavelength of some colours. Chromopuncture is a non-invasive technique born from a brilliant intuition of the German researcher Peter Mandel. Today he has a vast clinical case study to his credit and can boast important therapeutic successes and numerous awards in the academic field. The idea that in the form of light, and in particular of colours, it is possible to convey, through the acupuncture meridians, not so much energy but rather information, has today found a valid scientific foundation in the theory of biophotons of the German physicist Fritz Albert Popp .The application of a chromatic stimulus on the energy points identified transmits bioinformation which implements coordination processes at an organic and psychic level.

Chromopuncture does not act on the symptom, but aims to restore the basic energy balance. The operator places beams of colored light on the receptor points of the body, the same as in acupuncture or shiatsu or identified by P. Mandel. The points are stimulated by the specific electromagnetic frequencies emitted by the colored light. Chromopuncture does not act only on the symptom, but on its background, aiming to restore the energy/informational balance at the basis of a perfect homeostasis of biological processes in the human organism. Numerous scientific experiments have laid the foundations for a new science called photobiology, demonstrating that a light signal of a specific color (therefore wavelength), if it stimulates some biological molecules, catalyzes chemical reactions in which these molecules are normally involved, improving their effectiveness and speed. Furthermore, it has been demonstrated that the positive effects of light stimulation on cellular metabolism last over time.

This leads us to hypothesize that chromopuncture acts as a catalyst for biochemical reactions in order to optimize the activity of the central nervous system and the cascade of the immune, limbic and endocrine systems.

The scientific progress achieved in the last 40 years in this sector, starting from the joint research of Peter Mandel and Albert F. Popp, has made it possible to transfer much of the knowledge acquired in the health and wellness sector. The DEPT (Diagnosis Energy Point Terminal) known internationally as EEA (Energetic Emission Analysis), was developed by the German researcher Peter Mandel together with the German physicist A.F. Popp on the hypothesis that the emissions from the terminal points of the hands and feet, detected on photographic paper, were emissions of biophotons. Peter Mandel has identified the topographical correspondences between emissions and acupuncture meridians, organs, tissues, lived traumas. He does not give us information on the single symptom but highlights the cause by correlating it to the set of symptoms and constitutional tendencies.

The reading of a DEPT photo, carried out by specialized personnel, provides a holistic understanding of the predispositions and weaknesses present within the human system and, consequently, allows us to make hypotheses on the most suitable chromopuncture treatment for the person. Once the Chromopuncture treatment has been carried out, we proceed with a second DEPT detection, in order to evaluate the body's response to the light stimulus to which it has been subjected.

How do colors affect acupuncture points?

The different wavelengths emanating from the colors have the same action as the needles: in some cases they have a toning function, in others they are sedative, and act on the energy of our body. In short, their action is aimed at restoring the correct energy flow of the meridian to which that specific acupuncture point belongs to restore balance. The colors are red, yellow, orange, green, blue, indigo and violet.

Red, yellow and orange can be used to obtain a toning and exciting action, while blue is generally used to exert a more sedative action.

In chromopuncture, balance is represented by the color green. Inside, in fact, there are yellow and blue in equal proportion: the first represents the yang side of the activity, the blue instead the yin side. The action of chromopuncture, as well as that of acupuncture, aims to restore the lost balance. When this is missing, the body is unbalanced and characterized by the presence of full and empty energy and these are responsible for the appearance of the most varied disorders and pathologies of the organism, more or less serious. This is how chromopuncture works from a classic point of view. However, going to observe the action of chromopuncture from a more concrete and neurological point of view, what we observe is that the treatments we are talking about and the stimulation of certain points of the body, cause the body to release some neurotransmitters, chemical elements produced by the nervous system such as endorphins, serotonin and the like. They are the ones that determine the state of balance or imbalance of the organism. By stimulating certain points of the body in toning (for the production) or in energy dispersion (when faced with an excess of energy), all you do is give a plus or minus stimulus to the neurotransmitters. In short, on closer inspection, unlike classical medicine but also many other therapeutic strategies which involve the introduction of natural or synthetic substances into the body, through the action of reflexotherapy, the solution to a pathological problem is sought and found throughout within the organism itself.

The cure is inside the body, the purpose of the treatment is only to stimulate the body to produce what it itself needs to heal. Chromopuncture has a mechanism very similar to that of acupuncture as its basis of operation but in some cases it works better than the latter or at least it is more indicated. It is less invasive and does not involve penetrating the body with an object. Precisely because of this particularity, the chromopuncture treatment can also be carried out by specialists, not doctors, such as naturopaths or expert physiotherapists.

Given its minimally invasive nature, chromopuncture is more suitable than acupuncture as a treatment for children.

Just like in acupuncture, the great limitation of chromopuncture is represented by the intoxication from synthetic drugs that characterizes the body of each individual, which grows to a greater extent the more one goes on with age.

Chromopuncture makes use of the aid of various types of instruments capable of producing and directing the specific wavelengths of each color on the chosen point of the body. Generally the chromopunctor uses tools similar to pens, on the tip of which crystals are placed. In the past they were simple crystals which, subjected to the action of a light source, by breaking down the light, provided for the emanation of the wavelength of a specific colour. In more recent times halogen light "pens" have been produced inside which there are some colored filters similar to those used in photography: they are inserted and modulated for the different wavelengths characteristic of each color of the spectrum. The most modern version of the instrumentation used for chromopuncture treatments is the LED light, a light very similar to that of the laser. LED instruments are among all the most powerful ones. In some cases it is also possible to modify the frequency of the wavelengths of the colours, as already described: here is that the same color can perform different functions according to the frequency variations used for the stimulation of the points. Chromopuncture is also particularly suitable for the treatment of skeletal and muscle pathologies. In particular, auricular chromopuncture carries out an anti-inflammatory action against the problem through the stimulation of molecules secreted by the nerve fibers themselves, in this case cortisol, an endogenous cortisone that has a powerful anti-inflammatory action. Finally, there are general anti-inflammatory points on a somatic level (the master points).

- To treat inflammation, the most commonly used wavelengths are green (for muscles and tendons) and blue (for nerve inflammation). If a muscle has asthenia, the most commonly used colors are orange or red, colors and wavelengths capable of stimulating the part.

118

Each color has positive and negative properties and the preference of one color rather than another denotes specific psychic and behavioral characteristics. The best results in chromopuncture are obtained when stimulation using color wavelengths occurs on the points commonly used in auriculopuncture, a branch of acupuncture which is based on the stimulation of certain points located on the ear. In some cases, auricular chromopuncture is more effective than classic auricular puncture and the depth reached in the stimulation through colors is greater. During a somatic acupuncture treatment, as a rule and if it is well carried out, the patient does not feel pain; the auriculopuncture on the contrary normally arouses the sensation of pain, albeit bearable, in the points of the ear that correspond to the energetic area of the body affected by the pathology. When colors stimulate the ear points, the perceived pain is often more intense, as if the action of the wavelengths acted even deeper than the needles. This is a clear demonstration of the fact that the effect of the wavelengths (appropriately selected) of each color can sometimes be greater than the action of "classic" acupuncture and that is why it is believed that the point on the body where the chromopuncture finds greater application both in the ear. In fact, it is defined by oriental medicine as a small brain next to the real brain. It is based on the painful responses to the touch of the needles, or wavelengths in the case of chromotherapy, that the acupuncturist understands how to act.

Auricular acupuncture, and therefore also auricular chromopuncture, have a quicker and more immediate effect than somatic acupuncture. Reflexotherapy, in fact, has a direct action on the reticular substance, a portion of the brainstem located at the base of the brain. The ear is physically located very close to this point of the body, which is why the action of the ear chromopuncture will be much more immediate than the somatic variants of the technique.

Coopuncture can be used for:
- Strengthen the immune system.
- Detoxify the body.

- Restore strength and compactness to tissues, nails and hair.
- Restore luminosity and elasticity to the skin.
- Eliminate excess fat by harmonizing the vital functions of internal organs.
- Balance the entire endocrine system by reducing stress.
- Regulate wake-sleep, hunger-thirst cycles.

Chromopuncture acts directly on the seven organs of the brain (thalamus, hypothalamus, pineal and pituitary glands, corpus callosum, limbic system and medulla oblongata) and the results are visible and fast. This particular color treatment boasts several important therapeutic successes. The literature cites totally normalized conditions of hyperthyroidism and/or hypothyroidism, extreme food intolerances eliminated. In the case of children, chromopuncture works effectively in situations of insomnia or tormented nights, prolonged concentration difficulties and hyperactivity problems. Not only that: colic due to emotional problems, headaches, allergies. An effective and professional reality exists in Switzerland, in Locarno: it is the Chromopuncture Institute, where Dr. Neeresh has been practicing chromopuncture and has been teaching it to parents for years. With pediatric chromopuncture it is possible to treat the little ones through the principles of traditional Chinese medicine without incurring the inconvenience of the fear of needles frequent in children. The human eye can only perceive radiation between 4000 and 8000 Å (angstroms).
Each wavelength band corresponds to a color and has a specific therapeutic action when light is aimed at the skin through the interchangeable fiber optic pen:

- Red: 6200 Å (angstroms) = (620 nanometers). It is the decongestant color par excellence. Acts positively on the heart, lungs, muscles and restores physical energy.
- Orange: 5890 Å (angstroms) = (589 nanometers). It induces the person towards serenity, enthusiasm. Orange performs a stimulating action, awakens creativity.
- Yellow: 5510 Å (angstroms) = (551 nanometers). Yellow is connected to the digestive system. It helps recover the

biological rhythms, stimulates the appetite and the intellect.

- Green: 5120 Å (angstroms) = (512 nanometers). A color that acts as a sort of natural sedative. Green soothes the soul and, when applied to the skin, has a regenerating and positive action, especially on the endocrine system.
- Blue: 4750 Å (angstroms) = (475 nanometers). Blue balances breathing and heart rhythm, pushes subjects to dissolve those rigidities that lurk in the subconscious.
- Indigo: 4490 Å (angstroms) = (449 nanometers). Work on the mental state, increase inner calm and push towards thoughtful reasoning.
- Purple: 4230 Å (angstroms) = (423 nanometers). Connected to the right hemisphere, it balances spiritual energies and infuses psychophysical strength.

The qualities of the individual colors of the iris in aesthetic applications are:

- Red - It is called the great energetic; it is active in edema, temporary swelling, lymphatic and blood stasis. In the aesthetic field it is mainly used in cases of rough, intoxicated, edematous skin as well as in nodular cellulite (if not accompanied by circulatory imbalance).

- Orange - Symbolizes the rising sun. In aesthetics it is mainly used in the case of oily, young skin with an intermediate acneic tendency, comedonic skin, thick skin. It is active in dull and discolored epidermis; in imperfections (hypothenia, cellulite, adiposity) due to an imbalance in the digestive processes and altered functionality of the endocrine system. It works in cases of soft oedematous cellulite. Promotes hair shine; acts on greasy dandruff from sebaceous hypersecretion.

- Yellow - It is the color of rationality. In aesthetics it is mainly used in case of oily, asphyxiated, mature acneic skin and in lymphatic stasis. It is often active combined with other colors in impure skin with an acneic tendency, in asphyxiated, stressed and toneless epidermis. Activate the lymphatic system; cleanses the liver, intestines and skin and purifies the blood.

- Green - It is the color of serenity. In aesthetics it is mainly used in case of dry, alipic, relaxed withered, wrinkled, elderly, senescent, fragile, dehydrated skin. It is the building block of muscles and tissues. It is active in premature aging of the skin, wrinkles, sagging skin, undernutrition, dehydration, dyschromia. It works in cases of connective tissue weakness.

- Blue - It is the color of relaxation. In aesthetics, it is mainly used in the case of couperose skin, thin, with dilated pores, contracted, congested. It has antiseptic and bactericidal properties; it is soothing in burns and redness from heat. It acts on stress wrinkles and contracted features. It is also active in stress cellulite.

- Indigo - It is the color of sublimation. In aesthetics it is mainly used in the case of toneless, inelastic, pimply, sensitive, fissured skin. It is soothing in irritation due to prolonged sun exposure. Restores the natural tone to the fabrics. It is refreshing, astringent, haemostatic.

- Purple - It is the color of meditation. In aesthetics it is mainly used in the case of skin with freckles, with oxidation spots, presence of widespread oiliness. It is active in dermatosis in general. What you get with it is an increase in vascularization, which facilitates the work of the excretory organs, favoring the purification of the organism.

Chromotherapy massage

Color massage, or chromotherapy massage, is a useful experience for the body, mind and spirit as it allows us to rebalance our physical, energy and emotional levels in a single session. The chromotherapy massage uses color applied to the skin in an energetic key in the form of colored pigments conveyed in massage oils. Each of the seven colors has a different effect, affecting our physiological functions such as heart rate and fluid circulation, our emotional states, such as stress or depression, and our energy levels, associated with those in India called chakras. The chromotherapy massage combines all these characteristics; it takes place in a peaceful and comfortable context, where you can completely relax while the colors and the hands of the masseur do their job.

A fundamental tool used in chromotherapy massage is the frequency coming from the light; thanks to some lamps our body is irradiated directly where required or in the centers corresponding to the seven colours, acting with immediate effect and without filters on our energies. Furthermore, for the massage, blends of essential oils containing the same frequency of the color with which we want to work are used. The maneuvers include traditional physiotherapy techniques (joint mobilization, draining massage, muscle relaxant) and some holistic disciplines (such as reiki). However, the maneuvers are always performed in a gentle or moderately decisive manner, never such as to force the body to activate automatic defense mechanisms. The aim is to allow the frequencies of the oils and light to penetrate the tissues, allowing the energy centers to benefit from them.

The benefits obtained with the chromotherapy massage are as follows:
- Feeling of well-being and general health.
- Feeling of well-being and physical health.
- Emotional tranquility and clear mind.
- Unblocking some stagnant energies.

- Feeling of lightness and cleanliness.
- Feeling of greater inner balance.
- Drainage of liquids.
- Reduction of muscle tension.
- Freedom of joint movement.
- Reduction of any painful symptoms.

Massage is an ancient healing art that has been used for thousands of years, along with herbs and essential oils. The massage stimulates the immune system, digestion and assimilation of food are improved, blood and lymphatic circulation flow, muscles are toned, nerves are restored, the nervous system works better. From an emotional point of view these cuddles and caresses nourish us, they help us feel loved and accepted, building a healthy image of ourselves which is so vital for our physical, mental, emotional, spiritual functioning.
Today we know that stress is one of the primary causes of disease. High blood pressure, migraines, insomnia, depression, eating disorders, and substance abuse can wreak havoc on our bodies and minds. Massage teaches us to relax, it's a natural tranquilizer. Massage is no longer a simple gesture that creates pleasure for the body, but becomes a way to communicate more deeply with yourself. The massage transforms and becomes a journey into the awareness of the body, awakening dormant cellular memories and reminding them to act on the level of intelligence characteristics described for each single color.
The energy of Color speaks with Love to our body with seven different colored languages. Using these oils helps remind the body to provide Energy, Joy, Balance, Relaxation, Excitement and Freedom, releasing any emotions you want to let go.
Each color has therapeutic properties; the energy of color speaks lovingly to our body with seven different colored languages; using these oils helps remind the body to provide energy, joy, balance, relaxation, excitement and freedom, releasing all the emotions you want to let go.

- Orange: energy and joy for life with Melissa essential oil. Uplifts mood and relieves stress, reminds the body of the pleasure of living life in the broadest sense of the term.

- Red: energy for the body with Ylang Ylang essential oil, excellent for increasing energy, passion, love and self-confidence; allows you to intervene on cellulite and venous circulation.

- Yellow: stimulating energy for the body and mind with Rosemary essential oil, an excellent circulation stimulant that helps fight obesity and cellulite, toning the skin. Excellent mental stimulant, helps strengthen memory.

- Green: indicates the need for positivity; energy of love for the body with Eucalyptus essential oil. It has a rebalancing and calming effect. The oils associated with this color help the skin to oxygenate itself better.

- Blue: relaxing energy with Geranium essential oil. It has a relaxing and calming effect on body and mind.

- Violet: creative energy that leads to freedom, Lavender essential oil has calming, expanding and relaxing properties of well-being.

- Indigo: Energy that takes you to the stars, Patchouli essential oil has an aphrodisiac, uplifting effect and helps to abandon oneself and let go of anxieties.

We recommend using these essential oils mixed in a holly oil base. Holly oil is light, it is not absorbed deep into the skin, it has the task of transporting the essential oils, their message, and reaching the transmission code in the skin of the person being massaged.
Holly oil was discovered in 1993 and is produced in Canada. The characteristic of this massage oil is that it is a pure, clear, non-scented oil that leaves no stains and has an unlimited shelf life. It also has the characteristic of not causing allergic reactions and is not a seed-derived oil. It is a perfect carrier oil to be combined with essential oils and can also be stored on the shelf, even once opened. You don't have to worry about ambient

temperature or refrigeration because it has natural antibacterial properties.

Holly oil does not close pores or leave residue on the skin; its properties of lightness and transparency allow for less use of the product than sweet almond or grape seed oils. Finally, Holly oil does not stain fabrics or towels.

Benefits:
- Antibacterial.
- Antioxidant.
- Not scented.